ATTENTION-DEFICIT HYPERACTIVITY DISORDER:
A Clinical Workbook

RUSSELL A. BARKLEY, PhD
University of Massachusetts Medical Center

THE GUILFORD PRESS
New York   London

Contents

Preface

All of the materials in this manual are intended to be of utmost convenience and utility when employed in your clinical practice. They are taken from my recent text, *Attention-deficit Hyperactivity Disorder: A Handbook for Diagnosis and Treatment* (Guilford Press, 1990), which is recommended reading before using the enclosed materials clinically.

I am grateful to Dr. Arthur Robin for permission to use the Issues Checklist and Conflict Behavior Questionnaire, to Dr. George DuPaul for permission to use the ADHD Rating Scale and Academic Performance Rating Scale, to Dr. Craig Edelbrock for permission to use the Child Attention Profile, and to Drs. David Guevremont and David Dinklage for permission to use the Children's Atypical Development Scale. I am also indebted to the staff of the ADHD Clinic at the University of Massachusetts Medical Center for Assisting me in designing the ADHD Interview Form and to Drs. Sheldon Benjamin, Robert Kane, and Cecilia Mikalac for permission to use the Clinical Interview for Adult ADHD Patients and the related rating scales.

RUSSELL A. BARKLEY, PH.D.

ADHD Fact Sheet for Parents and Teachers

I have developed this fact sheet as a ready reference to be given to the parents and teachers of ADHD children seen in your clinical practice. It can be handed out to them as part of the feedback conference following an evaluation or mailed to school teachers along with more specific recommendations about the classroom management of the particular patient.

* * *

Attention-deficit Hyperactivity Disorder (ADHD) is the most recent term for a specific developmental disorder of both children and adults that is comprised of deficits in sustained attention, impulse control, and the regulation of activity level to situational demands. This disorder has had numerous different labels over the past century, including hyperkinetic reaction of childhood, hyperactivity or hyperactive child syndrome, minimal brain dysfunction, and Attention Deficit Disorder (with or without Hyperactivity).

MAJOR CHARACTERISTICS

The predominant features of this disorder are:

1. *Poor sustained attention or persistence of effort to tasks,* particularly those which are relatively tedious and protracted. This is frequently seen in the individual's becoming rapidly bored with repetitive tasks, shifting from one uncompleted activity to another, frequently losing concentration during lengthy tasks, and failing to complete routine assignments without supervision.

2. *Impaired impulse control or delay of gratification.* This is often noted in the individual's inability to stop and think before acting; to wait one's turn while playing or conversing with others; to work for larger, longer-term rewards rather than opting for smaller, immediate ones; and to inhibit behavior as a situation demands.

3. *Excessive task-irrelevant activity or activity poorly regulated to situational demands.* Individuals with ADHD are typically noted to be excessively fidgety, restless, and "on the go." They display excessive movement not required to complete a task, such as wriggling feet and legs, tapping things, rocking, or shifting position while performing relatively boring tasks. Trouble sitting still or inhibiting movement as a situation demands is often seen in younger children with ADHD.

4. *Deficient rule-following.* ADHD individuals frequently have difficulty following through on instructions or assignments, particularly without supervision. This is not due to poor language comprehension, defiance, or memory impairment. It seems as if instructions do not regulate behavior as well in ADHD individuals.

5. *Greater than normal variability during task performance.* Although there is not yet a consensus for including this characteristic with the others of ADHD, much research has accumulated to suggest that ADHD individuals show wide swings or considerably greater variation in the quality, accuracy, and speed with which they perform assigned work. This may be seen in highly variable school or work performance where the person fails to maintain a relatively even level of accuracy over time in performing repetitive or tedious tasks.

Although normal individuals, particularly young children, may show some of these features, what distinguishes the ADHD from normal individual is the considerably greater degree and frequency with which these characteristics are displayed.

OTHER CHARACTERISTICS

Several other features are associated with the disorder, these being:

1. *Early onset of the major characteristics.* Many ADHD individuals have demonstrated their problems since early childhood (mean age of onset is 3 to 4 years of age) and the vast majority have had their difficulties since 7 years of age.

2. *Situational variation.* The major characteristics show considerable situational variation in that the impairments are less likely to be seen in situations involving one-to-one activities with others, particularly if they are with their fathers or other authority figures. ADHD individuals also do better when the activities they are doing are novel, highly interesting, or involve an immediate consequence for completing them. Group situations or relatively repetitive, familiar, and uninteresting activities are likely to be most problematic for them.

3. *Relatively chronic course.* Most children with ADHD manifest their characteristics throughout childhood and adolescence. Although the major features improve with age, most ADHD individuals remain behind others their age in their ability to sustain attention, inhibit behavior, and regulate their activity level.

ADULT OUTCOME

It has been estimated that between 15% and 50% of children with ADHD ultimately outgrow their problems or at least achieve a point in life where their symptoms are no longer maladaptive. Most ADHD individuals will continue to display their characteristics into young adulthood. The professional literature has only recently recognized that adults may display these features as well, and may have manifested them since childhood. Between 35% and 60% of ADHD individuals will have problems with aggressiveness, conduct, and violation of legal or social norms during adolescence, and 25% are likely to become antisocial in adulthood. The most common area of maladjustment is in school work, where ADHD individuals are more likely to be retained in grade, provided special education, suspended for inappropriate conduct, expelled, or quit. ADHD individuals frequently have less educational attainment by adulthood than matched samples of normal individuals followed over the same time period. Approximately 35% of ADHD children will display a learning disability (i.e., delay in reading, math, spelling, writing, or language) beside their ADHD features. Among those ADHD individuals who develop conduct disorders or antisocial behavior in adolescence, substance abuse, especially using cigarettes and alcohol, are noted in the majority. ADHD individuals without conduct disorder show no greater tendency to substance abuse than do normal people.

FREQUENCY

ADHD occurs in approximately 3%–5% of the population, with a sex ratio of 3:1 (boys to girls). It is found in almost all countries and ethnic groups. It is more commonly seen in individuals with a history of conduct disorder, learning disabilities, or tics or Tourette's Syndrome.

ETIOLOGIES

ADHD appears to have a strong biological basis and is likely to be inherited in many cases. In others, it may be associated with greater-than-normal pregnancy or birth complications. In a few, it arises as a direct result of disease or trauma to the central nervous system. Research has not supported the popular views that ADHD is frequently due to the consumption of food additives, preservatives, or sugar. While a few ADHD individuals show an exacerbation of their features by allergies, these allergies are not viewed as the cause of ADHD. Individuals with seizures or epilepsy, or others who must take sedatives or anticonvulsant drugs, may develop ADHD as a side effect of their medication or find their preexisting ADHD features exacerbated by these medicines.

TREATMENT

No treatments have been found to cure this disability, but many exist that have shown some effectiveness in reducing the level of symptoms or the degree to which they impair adjustment. The most substantiated treatment is the use of stimulant medications. It is often recommended that other treatments be used before or in conjunction with the stimulant medications. These other treatments include training the parents of ADHD children in more effective child-management skills, modifying classroom behavior-management methods used by teachers, adjusting the length and number of assignments given to ADHD children at one time, and providing special educational services to ADHD children with more serious degrees of the disorder. Other treatments with some promise but not yet fully proven are social skills training, training in self-control methods, or use of antidepressant medication where stimulants are ineffective. For ADHD adults, providing vocational counseling, time management training, social skills counseling, and practical methods of coping with their disability may be helpful. The stimulant medications may be effective in the more severe cases.

Treatments with little or no evidence of their effectiveness include dietary management (elimination of sugar or food additives), long-term psychotherapy, high doses of vitamins, chiropractic treatment, or sensory-integration therapy—despite their widespread popularity.

The treatment of ADHD requires a comprehensive behavioral, psychological, educational, and sometimes medical evaluation followed by education of the individual or their caregivers as to the nature of the disorder and methods proven to assist with its management. Treatment is likely to be multidisciplinary, requiring the assistance of the mental health, educational, and medical professions at various points in its course. Treatment must be provided periodically over long time intervals in assisting ADHD individuals to cope with their behavioral disability.

Clinical Interview Form for Child and Adolescent ADHD Patients

This is the interview form that I and my colleagues use in the ADHD clinic at the University of Massachusetts Medical Center for interviewing parents of ADHD children. It contains questions pertaining to the child's developmental, medical, academic, and social histories as well as the current symptom lists for most of the childhood psychiatric disorders listed in the DSM-III-R. It is extremely useful for evaluating children and preparing subsequent clinical reports. It can also be used to set up a data base of information on clients in a computer file for use in clinical research projects.

ADHD CLINIC PARENT INTERVIEW

Name of Child _____   **Interview Date** _____

Interviewer _____   **Informant** _____

Patient No. _____

Reason for Referral:

Referral Source:

Parental Objectives:

I. DEVELOPMENTAL FACTORS
A. Prenatal History

1. How was your health during pregnancy?

Good ___ (1)
Fair ___ (3)
Poor ___ (5)
DK ___

2. How old were you when your child was born?

Under 20 ___ (1)
20–24 ___ (2)
25–29 ___ (3)
30–34 ___ (4)
35–39 ___ (5)
40–44 ___ (6)
Over 44 ___ (7)
DK ___

Do you recall using any of the following substances or medications during pregnancy?

3. Beer or wine
   (1) Never
   (2) Once or twice
   (3) 3–9 times
   (4) 10–19 times
   (5) 20–39 times
   (6) 40+ times

4. Hard liquor
   (1) Never
   (2) Once or twice
   (3) 3–9 times
   (4) 10–19 times
   (5) 20–39 times
   (6) 40+ times

5. Coffee or other caffeine (Cokes, etc.)
   Taken together, how many times?
   (1) Never
   (2) Once or twice
   (3) 3–9 times
   (4) 10–19 times
   (5) 20–39 times
   (6) 40+ times

6. Cigarettes
   (1) Never
   (2) Once or twice
   (3) 3–9 times
   (4) 10–19 times
   (5) 20–39 times
   (6) 40+ times

7. Did you ingest any of the following substances?
   ___ Valium (Librium, Xanax)
   ___ Tranquilizers
   ___ Antiseizure medications (e.g., Dilantin)
   ___ Treatment for diabetes
   ___ Antibiotics (for viral infections)
   ___ Sleeping pills
   ___ Other (please specify: _____)

B. Perinatal History

8. Did you have toxemia or eclampsia?

No ___ (0)
Yes ___ (1)
DK ___

9. Was there Rh factor incompatibility?

No ___ (0)
Yes ___ (1)
DK ___

10. Was (s)he born on schedule?

8 mos. or earlier ___ (1)
Term 8–10 mos. ___ (2)
10 mos. ___ (3)
DK ___

11. What was the duration of labor?

Under 6 hr ___ (1)
7–12 hr ___ (2)
13–18 hr ___ (3)
19–24 hr ___ (4)
Over 24 hr ___ (5)
DK ___

12. Were you given any drugs to ease the pain during labor?
Name: _____

No ___ (0)
Yes ___ (1)
DK ___

13. Were there indications of fetal distress during labor or during birth?

No ___ (0)
Yes ___ (1)
DK ___

14. Was delivery

Normal?

No ___ (0)
Yes ___ (1)

Breech?

No ___ (0)
Yes ___ (1)

Caesarian?

No ___ (0)
Yes ___ (1)

Forceps?

No ___ (0)
Yes ___ (1)

Induced?

No ___ (0)
Yes ___ (1)

15. What was the child's birth weight?

2 lb–3 lb 15 oz ___ (1)
4 lb–5 lb 15 oz ___ (2)
6 lb–7 lb 15 oz ___ (3)
8 lb–9 lb 15 oz ___ (4)
10 lb–11 lb 15 oz ___ (5)
DK ___

16. Were there any health complications following birth?

No ___ (0)
Yes ___ (1)

If yes, specify: _____

C. Postnatal Period and Infancy

17. Were there early infancy feeding problems?

No ___ (0)
Yes ___ (1)

18. Was the child colicky?

No ___ (0)
Yes ___ (1)

19. Were there early infancy sleep pattern difficulties?

No ___ (0)
Yes ___ (1)

20. Were there problems with the infant's responsiveness (alertness)?

No ___ (0)
Yes ___ (1)

21. Did the child experience any health problems during infancy?

No ___ (0)
Yes ___ (1)

22. Did the child have any congenital problems?

No ___ (0)
Yes ___ (1)

23. Was the child an easy baby? By that I mean did (s)he cry a lot? Did (s)he follow a schedule fairly well?

Very easy ___ (1)
Easy ___ (2)
Average ___ (3)
Difficult ___ (4)
Very diff. ___ (5)

24. How did the baby behave with other people?

More sociable than average ___ (1)
Average sociability ___ (2)
More unsociable than average ___ (3)

25. When (s)he wanted something, how insistent was (s)he?

Very insistent ___ (1)
Pretty insistent ___ (2)
Average ___ (3)
Not very insistent ___ (4)
Not at all insistent ___ (5)

26. How would you rate the activity level of the child as an infant/toddler?

Very active ___ (1)
Active ___ (2)
Average ___ (3)
Less active ___ (4)
Not active ___ (5)

D. Developmental Milestones

27. At what age did (s)he sit up?

3–6 mos. ___ (1)
7–12 mos. ___ (2)
Over 12 mos. ___ (3)
DK ___

28. At what age did (s)he crawl?

6–12 mos. ___ (1)
13–18 mos. ___ (2)
Over 18 mos. ___ (3)
DK ___

29. At what age did (s)he walk?

Under 1 yr ___ (1)
1–2 yr ___ (2)
2–3 yr ___ (3)
DK ___

30. At what age did (s)he speak single words (other than "mama" or "dada")?

9–13 mos. ___ (1)
14–18 mos. ___ (2)
19–24 mos. ___ (3)
25–36 mos. ___ (4)
37–48 mos. ___ (5)
DK ___

31. At what age did (s)he string two or more words together?

9–13 mos. ___ (1)
14–18 mos. ___ (2)
19–24 mos. ___ (3)
25–36 mos. ___ (4)
37–48 mos. ___ (5)
DK ___

32. At what age was (s)he toilet-trained? (Bladder control)

Under 1 yr ___ (1)
1–2 yr ___ (2)
2–3 yr ___ (3)
3–4 yr ___ (4)
DK ___

33. At what age was (s)he toilet-trained? (Bowel control)

Under 1 yr ___ (1)
1–2 yr ___ (2)
2–3 yr ___ (3)
3–4 yr ___ (4)
DK ___

34. Approximately how much time did toilet training take from onset to completion?

Less than 1 mo. ___ (1)
1–2 mos. ___ (2)
2–3 mos. ___ (3)
More than 3 mos. ___ (4)

II. MEDICAL HISTORY

35. How would you describe his/her health?

Very good ___ (1)
Good ___ (2)
Fair ___ (3)
Poor ___ (4)
Very poor ___ (5)

36. How is his/her hearing?

Good ___ (1)
Fair ___ (2)
Poor ___ (3)

37. How is his/her vision?

Good ___ (1)
Fair ___ (2)
Poor ___ (3)

38. How is his/her gross motor coordination?

Good ___ (1)
Fair ___ (2)
Poor ___ (3)

39. How is his/her fine motor coordination?

Good ___ (1)
Fair ___ (2)
Poor ___ (3)

40. How is his/her speech articulation?

Good ___ (1)
Fair ___ (2)
Poor ___ (3)

41. Has he had any chronic health problems (e.g., asthma, diabetes, heart condition)?

No ___ (0)
Yes ___ (1)

If yes, please specify: _____

42. When was the onset of any chronic illness?

Birth ___ (1)
0–1 yr ___ (2)
1–2 yr ___ (3)
2–3 yr ___ (4)
3–4 yr ___ (5)
Over 4 yr ___

43. Which of the following illnesses has the child had? (For the following, 0 = No; 1 = Yes)

Mumps ___
Chicken pox ___
Measles ___
Whooping cough ___
Scarlet fever ___
Pneumonia ___
Encephalitis ___
Otitis media ___
Lead poisoning ___
Seizures ___

Other diseases (specify): _____

44. Has the child had any accidents resulting in the following? (0 = No; 1 = Yes)

Broken bones ___
Severe lacerations ___
Head injury ___
Severe bruises ___
Stomach pumped ___
Eye injury ___
Lost teeth ___
Sutures ___

Other (specify): _____

45. How many accidents?

One ___ (1)
2–3 ___ (2)
4–7 ___ (3)
8–12 ___ (4)
Over 12 ___ (5)

46. Has he ever had surgery for any of the following conditions? (0 = No; 1 = Yes)

Tonsillitis ___
Adenoids ___
Hernia ___
Appendicitis ___
Eye, ear, nose, & throat ___
Digestive disorder ___
Urinary tract ___
Leg or arm ___
Burns ___
Other ___

47. How many times?

Once ___ (1)
Twice ___ (2)
3–5 times ___ (3)
6–8 times ___ (4)
Over 8 times ___ (5)

48. Duration of hospitalization?

One day   ___ (1)
One day + night ___ (2)
2–3 days   ___ (3)
4–6 days   ___ (4)
1–4 weeks   ___ (5)
1–2 mos.   ___ (6)
Over 2 mos.   ___ (7)

49. Is there any suspicion of alcohol or drug use?

No ___ (0)
Yes ___ (1)
DK ___

50. Is there any history of physical/sexual abuse?

No ___ (0)
Yes ___ (1)
DK ___

51. Does the child have any problems sleeping?

None   ___ (0)
Difficulty falling asleep   ___ (1)
Sleep continuity disturbance ___ (2)
Early morning awakening   ___ (3)

52. Is the child a restless sleeper?

No ___ (0)
Yes ___ (1)
DK ___

53. Does the child have bladder control problems . . . at night?

No ___ (0)
Yes ___ (1)

If yes, how often? _____
If yes, was (s)he ever continent? _____

. . . during the day?

No ___ (0)
Yes ___ (1)

If yes, how often? _____
If yes, was (s)he ever continent? _____

54. Does the child have bowel control problems . . . at night?

No ___ (0)
Yes ___ (1)

If yes, how often? _____
If yes, was (s)he ever continent? _____

. . . during the day?

No ___ (0)
Yes ___ (1)

If yes, how often? _____
If yes, was (s)he ever continent? _____

55. Does the child have any appetite control problems?

Overeats ___ (1)
Average ___ (2)
Undereats ___ (3)

III. TREATMENT HISTORY

56. Has the child ever been prescribed any of the following: (0 = No; 1 = Yes) (Duration coded in months)

Ritalin   ___   Tranquilizers   ___
Duration of use ___   Duration of use ___

Dexedrine	___	Anticonvulsants	___
Duration of use	___	Duration of use	___
Cylert	___	Antihistamines	___
Duration of use	___	Duration of use	___
		Other prescription drugs	___
		Duration of use	___
		Specify: _____	

57. Has the child ever had any of the following forms of psychological treatment? If so, how long did it last?

Individual psychotherapy	___
Duration of therapy	___
Group psychotherapy	___
Duration of therapy	___
Family therapy with child	___
Duration of therapy	___
Inpatient evaluation/Rx	___
Duration of inpatient stay	___
Residential treatment	___
Duration of placement	___

IV. SCHOOL HISTORY

Please summarize the child's progress (e.g., academic, social, testing) within each of these grade levels:

Preschool

Kindergarten

Grades 1 through 3

Grades 4 through 6

Grades 7 through 12

58. Has the child ever been in any type of special educational program, and if so, how long?

Learning disabilities class	___
Duration of placement	___
Behavioral/emotional disorders class	___
Duration of placement	___
Resource room	___
Duration of placement	___
Speech & language therapy	___
Duration of therapy	___
Other (please specify)	___
Duration	___

59. Has the child ever been:

Suspended from school	___	
Number of suspensions	___	
Expelled from school	___	
Number of expulsions	___	
Retained in grade	___	
Number of retentions	___	

60. Have any additional instructional modifications been attempted?

None	___	(0)
Behavior modification program	___	(1)
Daily/weekly report card	___	(2)
Other (please specify)	___	(3)

V. SOCIAL HISTORY

61. How does the child get along with his/her brothers/sisters?

Doesn't have any	___	(0)
Better than average	___	(1)
Average	___	(2)
Worse than average	___	(3)

62. How easily does the child make friends?

Easier than average	___	(1)
Average	___	(2)
Worse than average	___	(3)
DK	___	(4)

63. On the average, how long does your child keep friendships?

Less than 6 months	___	(1)
6 months–1 year	___	(2)
More than 1 year	___	(3)
DK	___	

VI. CURRENT BEHAVIORAL CONCERNS

<u>Primary concerns</u>   <u>Other (related) concerns</u>

64. What strategies have been implemented to address these problems? (Check which have been successful)

Verbal reprimands	___	(1)
Time out (isolation)	___	(2)
Removal of privileges	___	(3)
Rewards	___	(4)
Physical punishment	___	(5)
Acquiescence to child	___	(6)
Avoidance of child	___	(7)

65. On the average, what percentage of the time does your child comply with initial commands?

0–20%	___	(1)
20–40%	___	(2)
40–60%	___	(3)
60–80%	___	(4)
80–100%	___	(5)

66. On the average, what percentage of the time does your child eventually comply with commands?

0–20%	___ (1)
20–40%	___ (2)
40–60%	___ (3)
60–80%	___ (4)
80–100%	___ (5)

67. To what extent are you and your spouse consistent with respect to disciplinary strategies?

Most of the time	___ (1)
Some of the time	___ (2)
None of the time	___ (3)

68. Have any of the following stress events occurred within the past 12 months?

Parents divorced or separated	___ (1)
Family accident or illness	___ (2)
Death in family	___ (3)
Parent changed job	___ (4)
Changed schools	___ (5)
Family moved	___ (6)
Family financial problems	___ (7)
Other (please specify)	___ (8)

VII. DIAGNOSTIC CRITERIA

69. Which of the following are considered to be a significant problem at the present time? (0 = No; 1 = Yes)

Fidgets	___
Difficulty remaining seated	___
Easily distracted	___
Difficulty awaiting turn	___
Often blurts out answers to questions before they have been completed	___
Difficulty following instructions	___
Difficulty sustaining attention	___
Shifts from one activity to another	___
Difficulty playing quietly	___
Often talks excessively	___
Often interrupts or intrudes on others	___
Often does not listen	___
Often loses things	___
Often engages in physically dangerous activities	___

TOTAL FOR ADHD = ___ (8 or more)

70. When did these problems begin? (Specify age): ___

71. Which of the following are considered to be a significant problem at the present time. (0 = No; 1 = Yes)

Often loses temper	___
Often argues with adults	___
Often actively defies or refuses adult requests or rules	___
Often deliberately does things that annoy other people	___
Often blames others for own mistakes	___
Is often touchy or easily annoyed by others	___
Is often angry or resentful	___

15

Is often spiteful or vindictive ____
Often swears or uses obscene language ____

TOTAL for Oppositional Defiant Disorder = ____ (5 or more)

72. When did these problems begin? (Specify age): ____

73. Which of the following are considered to be a significant problem at the present time? (0 = No; 1 = Yes)

Stolen without confrontation ____
Run away from home overnight at least twice ____
Lies often ____
Deliberate fire-setting ____
Often truant ____
Breaking and entering ____
Destroyed others' property ____
Cruel to animals ____
Forced someone else into sexual activity ____
Used a weapon in a fight ____
Often initiates physical fights ____
Stolen with confrontation ____
Physically cruel to people ____

TOTAL for Conduct Disorder = ____ (3 or more)

74. When did these problems begin? (Specify age): ____

75. Which of the following are considered to be a significant problem at the present time? (0 = No; 1 = Yes)

Unrealistic and persistent worry about possible harm to attachment figures ____
Unrealistic and persistent worry that a calamitous event will separate the child from attachment figure ____
Persistent school refusal ____
Persistent refusal to sleep alone ____
Persistent avoidance of being alone ____
Repeated nightmares re: separation ____
Somatic complaints ____
Excessive distress in anticipation of separation from attachment figure ____
Excessive distress when separated from home or attachment figures ____

TOTAL for Separation Anxiety Disorder = ____ (3 or more)

76. When did these problems begin? (Specify age): ____

77. Which of the following are considered to be a significant problem at the present time? (0 = No; 1 = Yes)

Unrealistic worry about future events ____
Unrealistic concern about appropriateness of past behavior ____
Unrealistic concern about competence ____
Somatic complaints ____
Marked self-consciousness ____
Excessive need for reassurance ____
Marked inability to relax ____

TOTAL for Overanxious Disorder = ____ (4 or more)

78. When did these problems begin? (Specify age): ____

79. Which of the following are considered to be a significant problem at the present time? (0 = No; 1 = Yes)

Depressed or irritable mood most of day, nearly every day ___
Diminished pleasure in activities ___
Decrease or increase in appetite assoc. with possible failure to make weight gain ___
Insomnia or hypersomnia nearly every day ___
Psychomotor agitation or retardation ___
Fatigue or loss of energy ___
Feelings of worthlessness or excessive inappropriate guilt ___
Diminished ability to concentrate ___
Suicidal ideation or attempt ___

TOTAL for Major Depressive Episode (items 3–9) = ___ (5 or more)

80. When did these problems begin? (Specify age): ___

81. Which of the following are considered to be a significant problem at the present time? (0 = No; 1 = Yes)

Depressed or irritable mood for most of the day × 1 yr ___
Poor appetite or overeating ___
Insomnia or hypersomnia ___
Low energy or fatigue ___
Low self-esteem ___
Poor concentration or difficulty making decisions ___
Feelings of hopelessness ___
Never without symptoms for > 2 mos. over a 1-yr period ___

TOTAL for Dysthymia (items 2–7) = ___ (2 or more)

82. When did these problems begin? (Specify age): ___

VIII. OTHER CONCERNS

83. Has the child exhibited any of the symptoms below? (0 = No; 1 = Yes)

Stereotyped mannerisms ___
Odd postures ___
Excessive reaction to noise or fails to react to loud noises ___
Overreacts to touch ___
Compulsive rituals ___
Motor tics ___
Vocal tics ___

TOTAL = ___

(NOTE: The remaining questions in this section are optional.)

84. Has the child exhibited any symptoms of thought disturbance, including any of the following: (0 = No; 1 = Yes)

Loose thinking (e.g., tangential ideas, circumstantial speech) ___
Bizarre ideas (e.g., odd fascinations, delusions, hallucinations) ___
Disoriented, confused, staring, or "spacey" ___
Incoherent speech (mumbles, jargon) ___

TOTAL = ___

85. Has the child exhibited any symptoms of affective disturbance, including any of the following: (0 = No; 1 = Yes)

Excessive lability w/o reference to environ-
ment ___
Explosive temper with minimal provocation ___
Excessive clinging, attachment, or depen-
dence on adults ___
Unusual fears ___
Strange aversions ___
Panic attacks ___
Excessively constricted or bland affect ___
Situationally inappropriate emotions ___

TOTAL = ___

86. Has the child exhibited any symptoms of social conduct disturbance, including the following? (0 = No; 1 = Yes)

Little or no interest in peers ___
Significantly indiscreet remarks ___
Initiates or terminates interactions inappropriately ___
Qualitatively abnormal social behavior ___
Excessive reaction to changes in routine ___
Abnormalities of speech ___
Self-mutilation ___

TOTAL = ___

IX. FAMILY HISTORY

87. How long have you and the child's father (mother) been married? (Please note whether the child was the product of 1st, 2nd, etc. marriage.)

Never were married ___ (0)
Separated ___ (1)
Divorced ___ (2)
Widowed ___ (3)
Married for ___years ___ (4)

88. How stable is your current marriage?

Stable ___ (1)
Unstable ___ (2)

NOTES

PATERNAL RELATIVES

(0 = Negative; 1 = Positive)

	Self	Mother	Father	Siblings Bro	Bro	Sis	Sis	Total
Problems with aggressiveness, defiance, & oppositional behavior as a child								
Problems with attention, activity, & impulse control as a child								
Learning disabilities								
Failed to graduate from high school								
Mental retardation								
Psychosis or schizophrenia								
Depression for greater than 2 weeks								
Anxiety disorder that impaired adjustment								
Tics or Tourette's								
Alcohol abuse								
Substance abuse								
Antisocial behavior (assaults, thefts, etc.)								
Arrests								
Physical abuse								
Sexual abuse								

MATERNAL RELATIVES

(0 = Negative; 1 = Positive)

	Self	Mother	Father	Siblings Bro	Bro	Sis	Sis	Total
Problems with aggressiveness, defiance, & oppositional behavior as a child								
Problems with attention, activity, & impulse control as a child								
Learning disabilities								
Failed to graduate from high school								
Mental retardation								
Psychosis or schizophrenia								
Depression for greater than 2 weeks								
Anxiety disorder that impaired adjustment								
Tics or Tourette's								
Alcohol abuse								
Substance abuse								
Antisocial behavior (assaults, thefts, etc.)								
Arrests								
Physical abuse								
Sexual abuse								

SIBLINGS

(0 = Negative; 1 = Positive)

	Brother	Brother	Sister	Sister	Total
Problems with aggressiveness, defiance, & oppositional behavior as a child					
Problems with attention, activity, & impulse control as a child					
Learning disabilities					
Failed to graduate from high school					
Mental retardation					
Psychosis or schizophrenia					
Depression for greater than 2 weeks					
Anxiety disorder that impaired adjustment					
Tics or Tourette's					
Alcohol abuse					
Substance abuse					
Antisocial behavior (assaults, thefts, etc.)					
Arrests					
Physical abuse					
Sexual abuse					

Interview Form and Rating Scales for ADHD Adults

The following is the interview form that we use at the adult ADHD clinic at the University of Massachusetts Medical Center for evaluating adult referrals to our clinic. It is quite useful for the assessment of adults and the preparation of subsequent clinic reports. It can also be used to establish a data base in a computer file for later clinical research projects.

Also included here are the Self-Rating Symptom Checklist and Physical Complaints Checklist for conducting a quick screening of psychiatric and physical symptoms about which adult patients are currently concerned. The Patient's Behavior Checklist is also included to allow an assessment of adult ADHD symptoms. The items included in the scale were drawn from the DSM-III-R and were suggested by Rachel Gittelman and Paul Wender. These scales do not yet have norms for judging the degree of deviance of a patient's ratings but instead should simply be used as information-gathering tools about the client's current complaints.

SEMISTRUCTURED INTERVIEW FOR ADULT ADHD

Name _____   Date _____
Patient No. _____   Time _____
Date of Birth _____   Interviewer _____
Age _____

1. What led you to seek an evaluation for ADHD now?

2. What is your understanding of this disorder?

3. What do you know about the treatment of this disorder?

4. Do you know anyone else who was diagnosed with this disorder?
   1. Yes
   2. No
   3. Not sure

5. If yes, how were they treated for this disorder? (Circle any that apply)
   1. Ritalin or methylphenidate only
   2. Unknown medication or other medication only
   3. Therapy (group or individual) only
   4. Not sure how they were treated
   5. Other

   Comments:

6. What are your greatest concerns about your behavior now?

7. When would you say these problems began? (Circle any one)
   1. 0–7 years
   2. 8–12 years
   3. 13–15 years
   4. 16–21 years
   5. 22 to present

8. Now I'm going to ask you some symptoms, and I'd like you to tell me if they were ever more of a problem for you than for other people in your peer group.

Symptom	Yes	No	Now it is: Same	Better	Worse	Comments
a. Fidgetiness or feeling restless						
b. Difficulty remaining satisfied						
c. Being easily distracted						
d. Difficulty waiting your turn						
e. Blurting out answers before the question is completed						
f. Difficulty following through on or completing tasks						
g. Sustaining attention in tasks						

Symptom	Yes	No	Now it is: Same	Better	Worse	Comments
h. Frequently shifting from one task to another						
i. Difficulty doing tasks alone						
j. Talking too much						
k. Interrupting or intruding on others						
l. Not listening to others						
m. Losing important things or forgetting a lot						
n. Engaging in physically daring activities						
o. Always on the go, as if driven by a motor						
p. Making decisions too quickly or acting too quickly						
q. Impatient						

9. Did you ever seek treatment for these problems before? (Circle one)
   a. Yes
   b. No

   If yes, when and where did you seek treatment?

   What was the recommended treatment and the outcome?

10. Did your parents ever take you to see anyone about these problems when you were a child or adolescent?
    a. Yes
    b. No
    c. Not sure

11. Did your parents complain that you were difficult to control as a child?
    a. Yes
    b. No
    c. Not sure

    If yes, during what ages did they have this complaint? (Circle all that apply)
    a. 0–7 years
    b. 8–12
    c. 13–15
    d. 16–21
    e. 22+

12. Now I'm going to ask you some questions about school. What is the highest level of school that you have completed?
    a. 6th grade or less
    b. 7th or 8th grade
    c. Freshman or sophomore
    d. Junior high school
    e. Graduated from high school
    f. 1 or 2 years college
    g. 3 or 4 years college
    h. Postgraduate

13. Did you have any trouble starting school in kindergarten or first grade?

14. Did you ever repeat a grade?
    a. Yes
    b. No

    If yes, which grades did you repeat? _____

15. Were you ever in any special classes in school?
    a. Yes
    b. No

    If yes, what kinds of special classes were you in?

16. How would you describe your grades in school?

    a. Average

    b. Better than average

    c. Worse than average

17. What was your best subject in school? _____

18. What was your worst subject in school? _____

19. Did your teachers think you did as well as you could?

    a. Yes

    b. No

    c. Not sure

20. Were you ever truant from school?

    a. Yes

    b. No

If yes, how often and during what grades?

21. Were you ever expelled or suspended from school?

    a. Yes

    b. No

22. Did you ever get in any physical fights at school?

    a. Yes

    b. No

If yes:

    I. During which grades did you get into fights?

        a. K–6th grade

        b. 7th or 8th grade

        c. High school

        d. other

    II. How many times did you get into fights?

        a. One time

        b. Two to five times

        c. Six to ten times

        d. More than ten times

    III. Did you sometimes start the fight?

        a. Yes

        b. No

        c. Not sure

    IV. Did you ever use a weapon in a fight?

        a. Yes

        b. No

23. Did you ever run away from home overnight?

   a. Yes
   b. No

   If yes:

   I. How many times did you run away?
       a. Once
       b. Two to five times
       c. Six to ten times
       d. More than ten times

   II. What was the longest duration you ran away from home?
       a. One night
       b. Two to five nights
       c. Six to ten nights
       d. Longer than ten nights

24. Did you ever get in trouble for stealing or damaging property as a child or teenager?

   a. Yes
   b. No

25. Have you ever been arrested or in trouble with the law?

   a. Yes
   b. No

26. Do you have a driver's license?

   a. Yes
   b. No

   If yes:

   I. How many traffic tickets (not parking tickets) have you ever gotten?
       a. None
       b. One
       c. Two to three
       d. Four to five

   II. How many car accidents have you ever been in?
       a. None   d. Three
       b. One   e. Four or more
       c. Two

   If no: Why don't you have a driver's license?

27. Do you have problems with your temper?

   a. Yes
   b. No
   If yes, details:

28. Did you ever have any problems with your temper?

   a. Yes
   b. No
   c. Not sure

29. Have you ever lost your temper enough to hurt anyone or damage any property?

   a. Yes
   b. No

   If yes, details:

30. Do other people complain about your temper?

   a. Yes
   b. No
   c. Not sure

31. How would you describe your mood most of the time?

   a. Normal and fairly stable
   b. Anxious or nervous
   c. Depressed, sad, or blue
   d. Labile; mood changes a lot
   e. Other: _____

32. Do you have any problems with your sleep?

   a. Yes
   b. No

   If yes, details:

33. Do you have any problems with your weight?

   a. Yes
   b. No

   If yes, details:

34. Do you ever use any diet preparations?

   a. Yes
   b. No

   If yes, which ones?

35. How much alcohol do you drink *in a week?*

    a. I never drink   d. 5–10 drinks

    b. 0–1 drinks   e. More than 10

    c. 2–4 drinks

    Details:

36. Did you ever drink more heavily?

    a. Yes

    b. No

    If yes, details:

37. Have you ever used any drugs recreationally?

    a. Yes

    b. No

Drug	Used	Frequency
a. Pot, marijuana, hashish, grass		
b. Amphetamines, stimulants, uppers, speed		
c. Barbiturates, sedatives, downers, sleeping pills, Seconal, Quaaludes		
d. Tranquilizers, Valium, Librium		
e. Cocaine, coke, crack		
f. Heroin		
g. Opiates other than heroin (iodine, Demerol, morphine, methadone, Darvon, opium)		
h. Psychedelics (LSD, mescaline, peyote, DMT, PCP)		
i. Other (specify)		

38. Do you use any drugs recreationally now?

    a. Yes

    b. No

    If yes, what and how often?

39. Have you ever misused any prescription drugs?

    a. Yes

    b. No

    If yes, details:

PAST PSYCHIATRIC HISTORY

40. Have you ever seen a counselor or psychiatrist before?
    a. Yes
    b. No
    If yes, details:

41. Have you ever been hospitalized for a psychological or psychiatric problem?
    a. Yes
    b. No
    If yes, details:

42. Have you ever had problems with depression?
    a. Yes
    b. No
    If yes, details:

43. Have you ever had any problems with anxiety?
    a. Yes
    b. No
    If yes, details:

PAST MEDICAL HISTORY

44. Do you have any medical problems currently?
    a. Yes
    b. No
    If yes, details:

45. Have you ever been hospitalized medically?
    a. Yes
    b. No
    If yes, details:

46. Have you ever had any heart problems?
    a. Yes
    b. No
    If yes, details:

47. Have you ever had any liver disease?
    a. Yes
    b. No
    If yes, details:

48. Have you ever had glaucoma?
    a. Yes
    b. No
    If yes, details:

49. Have you ever had any seizures?
    a. Yes
    b. No
    If yes, details:

50. Do you have high blood pressure?
    a. Yes
    b. No
    If yes, details:

51. Are you ever troubled by chest pain or shortness of breath?
    a. Yes
    b. No
    If yes, details:

52. Have you ever had an injury to your head?

    a. Yes

    b. No

    If yes, details:

53. Have you ever lost consciousness?

    a. Yes

    b. No

    If yes, what was your first memory afterwards?
    Details:

54. Have you ever had encephalitis or a brain infection?

    a. Yes

    b. No

    If yes, details:

55. Have you ever had or do you now have any tics or unusual movements of your body?

    a. Yes

    b. No

    If yes, details:

56. Have you ever had or do you have any vocal tics, or do you make any unusal noises (Tourette's syndrome)?

    a. Yes

    b. No

    If yes, details:

57. Are you right-sided or left-sided (Insert R, L, Amb as appropriate)

    a. Writing _____   c. Throwing _____

    b. Kicking _____   d. Sighting _____

58. Have you ever had any problems with your thyroid gland?

    a. Yes

    b. No

    If yes, details:

DEVELOPMENTAL HISTORY

59. As far as you know, were there any problems with your mother's pregnancy or delivery of you?

    a. Yes

    b. No

    If yes, details:

60. As far as you know, did you walk, talk, and sit up on time?

    a. Yes

    b. No

    If no, details:

61. Did you have any childhood illnesses?

    a. Yes

    b. No

    If yes, details:

62. Did you have normal relationships with your peers when you were a child?

    a. Yes

    b. No

    If no, details:

SEXUAL HISTORY (for Females Only)

63. Are you sexually active?

    a. Yes

    b. No

64. Are you trying to get pregnant?

    a. Yes

    b. No

65. Do you intend to get pregnant within the next 5 years?

    a. Yes

    b. No

66. Are you using any birth control?

    a. Yes

    b. No

67. Are you currently nursing?

    a. Yes

    b. No

MEDICATIONS

68. Do you take any medications?

    a. Yes

    b. No

    If yes, details:

69. Do you take any over-the-counter medications?

    a. Yes

    b. No

    If yes, details:

70. (For women) Do you use birth control pills?

    a. Yes

    b. No

ALLERGIES

71. Do you have any allergies to medications?

    a. Yes

    b. No

    If yes, details:

72. Do you have any other allergies?

    a. Yes

    b. No

    If yes, details:

FAMILY HISTORY

73. Are there any medical illnesses that run in your family?

    a. Yes

    b. No

    If yes, details:

74. Is there anyone in your family who has had problems with anxiety or depression?

    a. Yes

    b. No

    If yes, details:

75. Is there anyone in your family who has abused alcohol or other drugs?

    a. Yes

    b. No

    If yes, details:

76. Is there anyone in your family who has had any psychiatric illness?

    a. Yes

    b. No

    If yes, details:

77. Is there anyone in your family who has been in trouble with the law?

    a. Yes

    b. No

    If yes, details:

78. Is there anyone in your family who has had seizures or other neurological problems?
    a. Yes
    b. No
    If yes, details:

79. Is there anyone in your family who has had Tourette's syndrome or vocal tics?
    a. Yes
    b. No
    If yes, details:

80. Is there anyone in your family who has a movement disorder or any unusual movements?
    a. Yes
    b. No
    If yes, details:

81. Is there anyone in your family who has had heart problems?
    a. Yes
    b. No
    If yes, details:

82. Is there anyone in your family who has high blood pressure?
    a. Yes
    b. No
    If yes, details:

83. Is there anyone in your family who has had attentional problems?
    a. Yes
    b. No
    If yes, details:

84. Is there anyone in your family who has had learning disabilities?

   a. Yes
   b. No

   If yes, details:

SOCIAL HISTORY

85. How much do you smoke?

   a. Never smoked
   b. Have quit for more than a year
   c. Have quit for less than a year
   d. Less than half a pack per day (ppd)
   e. Half to one ppd
   f. One to two ppd
   g. Two or more ppd

86. How much caffeine do you drink, including caffeinated tea and soda?

   a. None
   b. 1–2 cups per day
   c. 3–4 cups per day
   d. 5–6 cups per day
   e. 7–10 cups per day
   f. 11+ cups per day

87. Can you tell me your work history, starting as far back as you can remember?

88. Have you served in the military?

   a. Yes
   b. No

   If yes, details (highest rank, special honors, duties, discharge status):

89. What is your current marital status?

   a. Never married
   b. Married
   c. Separated
   d. Divorced
   e. Widowed

90. Are you currently in an intimate relationship?

   a. Yes
   b. No

   If yes, for how long?

   a. Less than 3 months
   b. 3–6 months
   c. 7 months–1 year
   d. 1–5 years
   e. 5–10 years
   f. 10+ years

91. Do you have trouble in your relationships with others?

    a. Yes
    b. No

    If yes, details:

92. How many intimate relationships have you had that lasted more than 3 months?

    a. None   c. Three or four
    b. One or two   d. Five or more

93. I have asked you a lot of questions. Can you think for a minute and tell me if there are any other problems you have that might be related to what you came here for?

SELF-RATING SYMPTOM CHECKLIST FOR ADHD ADULTS

Name _____   **Date** _____

Please rate the degree to which you have been experiencing the following problems during the PAST WEEK by making an "X" across each of the following lines:

	Not a problem									Very severe problem

1. Anxiety

   0   1   2   3   4   5   6   7   8   9   10

2. Depression

   0   1   2   3   4   5   6   7   8   9   10

3. Disturbing thoughts

   0   1   2   3   4   5   6   7   8   9   10

4. Fears/fearfulness

   0   1   2   3   4   5   6   7   8   9   10

5. Angry outbursts (temper)

   0   1   2   3   4   5   6   7   8   9   10

6. Eating problems

   0   1   2   3   4   5   6   7   8   9   10

   Specify _____

7. Sleep problems

   0   1   2   3   4   5   6   7   8   9   10

   Specify _____

8. Fatigue

   0   1   2   3   4   5   6   7   8   9   10

9. Sexual problems

   0   1   2   3   4   5   6   7   8   9   10

   Specify _____

10. Alcohol and/or drug problems

   0   1   2   3   4   5   6   7   8   9   10

   Specify _____

11. Stress

   0   1   2   3   4   5   6   7   8   9   10

	Not a problem										Very severe problem
12. Work/school problems	0	1	2	3	4	5	6	7	8	9	10
13. Family problems	0	1	2	3	4	5	6	7	8	9	10
14. Child-rearing problems	0	1	2	3	4	5	6	7	8	9	10
15. Problems getting along w/others	0	1	2	3	4	5	6	7	8	9	10
16. Violence	0	1	2	3	4	5	6	7	8	9	10

Specify _____

17. Health problems	0	1	2	3	4	5	6	7	8	9	10

Specify _____

18. Legal problems	0	1	2	3	4	5	6	7	8	9	10
19. Financial problems	0	1	2	3	4	5	6	7	8	9	10
20. Other problem	0	1	2	3	4	5	6	7	8	9	10

Specify _____

21. Other problem	0	1	2	3	4	5	6	7	8	9	10

Specify _____

22. Other problem	0	1	2	3	4	5	6	7	8	9	10

Specify _____

Please circle the numbers of *UP TO THREE* problems that you consider to be your *MAIN* problem(s).

PHYSICAL COMPLAINTS CHECKLIST FOR ADHD ADULTS

Name _____

Date _____

Below is a list of symptoms that some people have. Beside each item indicate how often each is a problem for you.

	Never	Less than 4 times/yr	Less than once/mo.	Less than once/wk	1–3 times/wk	Nearly daily
1. Headaches						
2. Trouble sleeping						
3. Irritable, nervous						
4. Stomach upset						
5. Aches and pains (not backache)						
6. Backache						
7. Rapid heartbeat						
8. Dizziness/lightheadedness						
9. Vomiting, nausea						
10. Diarrhea						
11. Constipation						
12. Weakness						
13. Tired during the day						
14. Poor appetite						
15. Blurred vision						
16. Dry mouth						
17. Confusion						

PATIENT'S BEHAVIOR CHECKLIST FOR ADHD ADULTS

Name _____

Date _____

Below is a list of problems and behaviors that some patients have. Beside each item indicate how much of a problem each one is for you in *your* opinion.

	Not at all	Just a little	Pretty much	Very much
1. Physical restlessness				
2. Mental restlessness				
3. Easily distracted				
4. Impatient				
5. "Hot" or explosive temper				
6. Unpredictable behavior				
7. Difficulty completing tasks				
8. Shifting from one task to another				
9. Difficulty sustaining attention				
10. Impulsive				
11. Talks too much				
12. Difficulty doing tasks alone				
13. Often interrupts others				
14. Doesn't appear to listen to others				
15. Loses a lot of things				
16. Forgets to do things				
17. Engages in physically daring activities				
18. Always on the go, as if driven by a motor				

ADHD Rating Scale

This rating scale was developed by myself and Dr. George DuPaul for evaluating the occurrence of ADHD symptoms in children. We took the 14 items for ADHD from the DSM-III-R and placed them in a rating scale format. We then collected norms on a large sample of children from central Massachusetts. The scale, scoring instructions, and norms are provided. The scale can be completed by both parents and teachers. Generally, we calculate the following scores:

1. *Number of symptoms present.* Simply add the number of items rated as 2 or higher. A score of 8 or more exceeds the DSM-III-R cutoff for a diagnosis of ADHD.

2. *Total score.* Sum the total number of points for all 14 items. If the score exceeds 1.5 standard deviations above the mean for age and sex (see tables), it is a clinically significant score.

3. *Factor I: Inattentive–Hyperactive.* Sum the items for this factor as shown on the next page and compare the score to the table of norms for the child's age and sex. Again, a score higher than 1.5 standard deviations above the mean indicates a clinically significant problem in the area of inattention.

4. *Factor II: Impulsive–Hyperactive.* Sum the items for this factor as shown on the next page and compare the score to the table of norms for the child's age and sex. Again, a score higher than 1.5 standard deviations above the mean indicates a clinically significant problem in the area of impulsivity.

ADHD RATING SCALE

Child's Name _____ **Age** _____ **Grade** _____
Completed by _____

Circle the number in the *one* column which best describes the child.

	Not at all	Just a little	Pretty much	Very much
1. Often fidgets or squirms in seat.	0	1	2 -	3
2. Has difficulty remaining seated.	0	1	2	3
3. Is easily distracted.	0	1	2	3
4. Has difficulty awaiting turn in groups.	0	1	2	3
5. Often blurts out answers to questions.	0	1	2	3
6. Has difficulty following instructions.	0	1	2	3
7. Has difficulty sustaining attention to tasks.	0	1	2	3
8. Often shifts from one uncompleted activity to another.	0	1	2	3
9. Has difficulty playing quietly.	0	1	2	3
10. Often talks excessively.	0	1	2	3
11. Often interrupts or intrudes on others.	0	1	2	3
12. Often does not seem to listen.	0	1	2	3
13. Often loses things necessary for tasks.	0	1	2	3
14. Often engages in physically dangerous activities without considering consequences.	0	1	2	3

Note. From *The ADHD Rating Scale: Normative Data, Reliability, and Validity* by G. J. DuPaul, 1990, unpublished manuscript, University of Massachusetts Medical Center, Worcester. Reprinted by permission of the author. This form may be reproduced for personal use.

SCORING INSTRUCTIONS: ADHD RATING SCALE

Parent Ratings

Total score: Sum items 1–14.
Inattention–Hyperactivity: Sum items 1–3, 6–8, 12–14.
Impulsivity–Hyperactivity: Sum items 1, 2, 4, 5, 9–11, 14.

Teacher Ratings

Total score: Sum items 1–14.
Inattention–Hyperactivity: Sum items 1–3, 6–8, 12, 13.
Impulsivity–Hyperactivity: Sum items 1, 2, 4, 5, 9–11, 14.

MEANS AND STANDARD DEVIATIONS FOR PARENT-COMPLETED ADHD RATING SCALE BY GENDER AND AGE

Age	Boys			Girls		
	Total	Factor I	Factor II	Total	Factor I	Factor II
6 years (*n* = 113)						
M	13.71	8.54	8.08	11.50	7.18	6.56
SD	9.66	6.58	5.70	9.51	6.42	5.44
7 years (*n* = 117)						
M	13.69	8.96	7.69	10.65	6.67	5.83
SD	11.89	8.06	6.90	8.95	5.72	5.08
8 years (*n* = 108)						
M	16.21	10.70	8.96	10.92	6.92	5.77
SD	10.97	7.60	6.01	8.71	5.97	4.72
9 years (*n* = 94)						
M	14.08	9.19	7.65	11.23	7.26	5.93
SD	10.40	7.11	6.08	9.27	6.34	4.96
10 years (*n* = 105)						
M	13.71	9.65	6.73	10.68	6.64	5.66
SD	10.22	7.75	5.25	10.18	6.39	6.01
11 years (*n* = 80)						
M	13.91	9.22	7.34	7.34	4.63	3.63
SD	11.69	8.08	6.58	9.25	6.06	4.90
12 years (*n* = 52)						
M	15.34	10.79	7.21	7.70	5.22	3.65
SD	10.72	7.59	5.57	10.15	6.42	5.69

Note. From *The ADHD Rating Scale: Normative Data, Reliability, and Validity* by G. J. DuPaul, 1990, unpublished manuscript, University of Massachusetts Medical Center, Worcester. Reprinted by permission of the author.

MEANS AND STANDARD DEVIATIONS FOR TEACHER-COMPLETED ADHD RATING SCALE BY GENDER AND AGE

Age	Boys			Girls		
	Total	Factor I	Factor II	Total	Factor I	Factor II
6 years (*n* = 55)						
M	12.04	7.88	6.19	8.69	5.83	4.31
SD	12.17	7.60	6.64	9.88	5.97	5.87
7 years (*n* = 89)						
M	13.46	8.41	7.17	10.47	7.12	5.40
SD	11.52	7.58	7.65	11.37	7.36	6.10
8 years (*n* = 102)						
M	10.81	6.52	6.00	8.54	6.00	3.86
SD	9.94	6.23	5.94	9.36	6.21	5.26
9 years (*n* = 89)						
M	13.46	8.17	7.34	9.67	5.85	5.21
SD	12.41	7.51	7.09	10.22	6.26	6.13
10 years (*n* = 84)						
M	11.82	7.67	5.82	7.44	5.15	3.34
SD	10.46	6.98	5.92	8.44	6.10	4.44
11 years (*n* = 96)						
M	13.98	8.93	6.90	7.18	4.36	3.78
SD	13.25	7.81	7.71	9.29	5.71	5.51
12 years (*n* = 36)						
M	12.10	7.05	6.50	7.19	4.75	3.31
SD	8.12	5.55	4.54	8.14	5.22	4.32

Note. From *The ADHD Rating Scale: Normative Data, Reliability, and Validity* by G. J. DuPaul, 1990, unpublished manuscript, University of Massachusetts Medical Center, Worcester. Reprinted by permission of the author.

Child Attention Profile

The Child Attention Profile (CAP) was developed by Craig Edelbrock, Ph.D., as a convenient means of briefly assessing the presence and degree of inattention and overactivity in children as reported by teachers. The items were drawn from the Child Behavior Checklist–Teacher Report Form as were the normative data reported here. We have used the scale not only for assessing symptoms of ADHD in children, but also for distinguishing Attention Deficit Disorder with Hyperactivity (ADD + H) from children with Attention Deficit Disorder without Hyperactivity (ADD – H). In our research on these subgroups, we typically classified a child who placed above the 93rd percentile on both the inattention and overactivity scales of the CAP as having ADD + H. Those children having scores on inattention over the 93rd percentile but scores on overactivity less than the 84th percentile were classified as ADD – H.

ADMINISTRATION

The CAP was designed to be completed by teachers or teacher aides on a weekly basis.

SCORING

Each item is scored 0 for *Not True,* 1 for *Somewhat* or *Sometimes True,* or 2 for *Very* or *Often True.* Total Score is the sum of all 12 items (range: 0–24). Upper limit of the normal range is 15 for boys, 11 for girls. Inattention is the sum of items 1, 2, 5, 7, 9, 10, & 12 (range: 0–14). Upper limit of the normal range is 9 for boys, 7 for girls. Overactivity is the sum of items 3, 4, 6, 8 & 11 (range 0–10). Upper limit of the normal range is 6 for boys, 5 for girls.

CHILD ATTENTION PROFILE

Child's Name _____ **Child's Age** _____

Filled Out by _____ **Child's Sex** [ ] M [ ] F

Directions: Below is a list of items that describe pupils. For each item that describes the pupil *now* or *within the past week,* check whether the item is *Not True, Somewhat* or *Sometimes True,* or *Very* or *Often True.* Please check all items as well as you can, even if some do not seem to apply to this pupil.

	Not true	Somewhat or sometimes true	Very or often true
1. Fails to finish things he/she starts	[ ]	[ ]	[ ]
2. Can't concentrate, can't pay attention for long	[ ]	[ ]	[ ]
3. Can't sit still, restless, or hyperactive	[ ]	[ ]	[ ]
4. Fidgets	[ ]	[ ]	[ ]
5. Daydreams or gets lost in his/her thoughts	[ ]	[ ]	[ ]
6. Impulsive or acts without thinking	[ ]	[ ]	[ ]
7. Difficulty following directions	[ ]	[ ]	[ ]
8. Talks out of turn	[ ]	[ ]	[ ]
9. Messy work	[ ]	[ ]	[ ]
10. Inattentive, easily distracted	[ ]	[ ]	[ ]
11. Talks too much	[ ]	[ ]	[ ]
12. Fails to carry out assigned tasks	[ ]	[ ]	[ ]

Please feel free to write any comments about the pupil's work or behavior in the last week.

Note. From C. S. Edelbrock. University of Massachusetts Medical Center, Worcester. Reprinted by permission. This form may be reproduced for personal use.

NORMATIVE CUTOFF POINTS FOR THE INATTENTION, OVERACTIVITY, AND TOTAL SCORES FOR THE CHILD ATTENTION PROFILE

Cutoff points	Total (1,100)[a]	Boys (550)	Girls (550)
	Inattention[b]		
Median	1	2	0
69th percentile	3	4	2
84th percentile	6	7	5
93rd percentile	8	9	7
98th percentile	11	12	10
	Overactivity		
Median	0	1	0
69th percentile	1	2	1
84th percentile	4	4	2
93rd percentile	6	6	5
98th percentile	8	8	7
	Total score		
Median	2	4	1
69th percentile	6	7	4
84th percentile	10	11	8
93rd percentile	14	15	11
98th percentile	19	20	16

Note. From C. S. Edelbrock, Dept. of Psychiatry, University of Massachusetts Medical Center, Worcester. Reprinted by permission.

[a] Numbers in parentheses are sample sizes.

[b] The inattention score is the sum of items 1, 2, 5, 7, 9, 10, and 12. The Overactivity score is the sum of items 3, 4, 6, 8, and 11. Table entries are raw scores that fall at or below the designated percentile range. The 93rd percentile is the recommended upper limit of the normal range. Scores exceeding this cutoff are in the clinical range. All scores are based on teacher reports.

Original Home and School Situations Questionnaires

These rating scales were designed by me to assess the different situations in which children may present with behavior problems at home and school. Consequently, these scales are most useful for obtaining information about defiant, aggressive, or oppositional behavior. Although they may also be used to evaluate children with ADHD, the revised HSQ and SSQ described in the next section of this manual are probably better for this purpose as the instructions pertain more specifically to attention problems. Norms are provided for each rating scale.

You can obtain two scores for each rating scale:

the number of problem settings and the mean severity score. They are obtained by doing the following:

1. *Number of problem settings*. Count the number of Yes answers.
2. *Mean severity*. Sum the circled numbers and divide by the number of Yes answers.

Compare the child's scores to those provided in the tables of norms. Any child whose score is greater than 1.5 standard deviations above the mean (93rd%) for their age and sex is considered to be deviant on this scale.

HOME SITUATIONS QUESTIONNAIRE

Child's Name _____ **Date** _____

Name of Person Completing This Form _____

Instructions: Does your child present any problems with compliance to instructions, commands, or rules for you in any of these situations? If so, please circle the word Yes and then circle a number beside that situation that describes how severe the problem is for you. If your child is not a problem in a situation, circle No and go on to the next situation on the form.

Situations	Yes/No (Circle one)		If yes, how severe? Mild (Circle one) Severe
Playing alone	Yes	No	1 2 3 4 5 6 7 8 9
Playing with other children	Yes	No	1 2 3 4 5 6 7 8 9
Mealtimes	Yes	No	1 2 3 4 5 6 7 8 9
Getting dressed/undressed	Yes	No	1 2 3 4 5 6 7 8 9
Washing and bathing	Yes	No	1 2 3 4 5 6 7 8 9
When you are on the telephone	Yes	No	1 2 3 4 5 6 7 8 9
Watching television	Yes	No	1 2 3 4 5 6 7 8 9
When visitors are in your home	Yes	No	1 2 3 4 5 6 7 8 9
When you are visiting someone's home	Yes	No	1 2 3 4 5 6 7 8 9
In public places (restaurants, stores, church, etc.)	Yes	No	1 2 3 4 5 6 7 8 9
When father is home	Yes	No	1 2 3 4 5 6 7 8 9
When asked to do chores	Yes	No	1 2 3 4 5 6 7 8 9
When asked to do homework	Yes	No	1 2 3 4 5 6 7 8 9
At bedtime	Yes	No	1 2 3 4 5 6 7 8 9
While in the car	Yes	No	1 2 3 4 5 6 7 8 9
When with a babysitter	Yes	No	1 2 3 4 5 6 7 8 9

------------------------------------ For Office Use Only ------------------------------------

Total number of problem settings _____ Mean severity score _____

SCHOOL SITUATIONS QUESTIONNAIRE

Child's Name _____ **Date** _____

Name of Person Completing This Form _____

Does this child present any behavior problems for you in any of these situations? If so, indicate how severe they are.

Situations	Yes/No (Circle one)		Mild	If yes, how severe? (Circle one)							Severe
While arriving at school	Yes	No	1	2	3	4	5	6	7	8	9
During individual deskwork	Yes	No	1	2	3	4	5	6	7	8	9
During small-group activities	Yes	No	1	2	3	4	5	6	7	8	9
During free-play time in class	Yes	No	1	2	3	4	5	6	7	8	9
During lectures to the class	Yes	No	1	2	3	4	5	6	7	8	9
At recess	Yes	No	1	2	3	4	5	6	7	8	9
At lunch	Yes	No	1	2	3	4	5	6	7	8	9
In the hallways	Yes	No	1	2	3	4	5	6	7	8	9
In the bathroom	Yes	No	1	2	3	4	5	6	7	8	9
On field trips	Yes	No	1	2	3	4	5	6	7	8	9
During special assemblies	Yes	No	1	2	3	4	5	6	7	8	9
On the bus	Yes	No	1	2	3	4	5	6	7	8	9

-------------------------------------- For Office Use Only --------------------------------------

Total number of problem settings _____ Mean severity score _____

Note. From *Defiant Children: A Clinician's Manual for Parent Training* by R. A. Barkley, 1987, New York: Guilford Press. Copyright 1987 by The Guilford Press. A Division of Guilford Publications, Inc. This form may be reproduced for personal use.

NORMS FOR THE HOME SITUATIONS
QUESTIONNAIRE (HSQ)

Age groups (in years)	n	Number of problem settings	Mean severity
Boys			
4–5	162	3.1 (2.8)	1.7 (1.4)
6–8	205	4.1 (3.3)	2.0 (1.4)
9–11	138	3.6 (3.3)	1.9 (1.5)
Girls			
4–5	146	2.2 (2.6)	1.3 (1.4)
6–8	202	3.4 (3.5)	1.6 (1.5)
9–11	142	2.7 (3.2)	1.4 (1.4)

Note. Table entries are means with standard deviations in parentheses. From *Factor Structures of the Home Situations Questionnaire (HSQ) and the School Situations Questionnaire (SSQ)* by M. J. Breen and T. S. Altepeter, 1990, unpublished manuscript, Winneconne Public Schools, Winneconne, WI. Reprinted by permission of the author.

NORMS FOR THE SCHOOL SITUATIONS
QUESTIONNAIRE (SSQ)

Age groups (in years)	n	Number of problem settings	Mean severity
Boys			
6–8	170	2.4 (3.3)	1.5 (2.0)
9–11	123	2.8 (3.2)	1.9 (2.1)
Girls			
6–8	180	1.0 (2.0)	0.8 (1.5)
9–11	126	1.3 (2.1)	0.8 (1.2)

Note. Table entries are means with standard deviations in parentheses. From *Factor Structures of the Home Situations Questionnaire (HSQ) and the School Situations Questionnaire (SSQ)* by M. J. Breen and T. S. Altepeter, 1990, unpublished manuscript, Winneconne Public Schools, Winneconne, WI. Reprinted by permission of the authors.

Revised Home and School Situations Questionnaires

These revisions of the HSQ and SSQ were created to permit parents and teachers to rate specific problems children might have with attention or concentration. As a result, the revised scales are most useful for evaluating children in whom a concern about ADHD or ADD without Hyperactivity is the major referral issue.

You can obtain four scores for the HSQ–R and two for the SSQ–R rating scale: the number of problem settings and the mean severity score. They are obtained by doing the following:

1. *Number of problem settings.* Count the number of Yes answers.

2. *Mean severity.* Sum the circled numbers and divide by the number of Yes answers.

3. *Factor I: Compliance Situations.* Sum the items listed in the scoring instructions for Factor I.

4. *Factor II: Leisure Situations.* Sum the items shown in the scoring instructions for Factor II.

Compare the child's scores to those provided in the tables of norms. Any child whose score is greater than 1.5 standard deviations above the mean (93rd%)

for their age and sex is considered to be deviant on this scale.

SCORING INSTRUCTIONS: REVISED SITUATIONS QUESTIONNAIRES

Home Situations Questionnaire—Revised

Number of problem settings: Sum of Yes responses to all items.
Mean severity: Sum of severity ratings divided by the number of Yes responses.
Factor I: Sum severity rating (0–9) for items 3, 4, 6–11, 13, 14.
Factor II: Sum severity rating (0–9) for items 1, 2, 5–7, 11–13.

School Situations Questionnaire—Revised

Number of problem settings: Sum of Yes responses to all items.
Mean severity: Sum of severity ratings divided by the number of Yes responses.

HOME SITUATIONS QUESTIONNAIRE—REVISED

Name of Child _____ **Date** _____

Name of Person Completing This Form _____

Does this child have problems paying attention or concentrating in any of these situations? If so, indicate how severe these attentional difficulties are.

Situations	Yes/No (Circle one)		If yes, how severe? Mild (Circle one) Severe
While playing alone	Yes	No	1 2 3 4 5 6 7 8 9
While playing with other children	Yes	No	1 2 3 4 5 6 7 8 9
Mealtimes	Yes	No	1 2 3 4 5 6 7 8 9
Getting dressed	Yes	No	1 2 3 4 5 6 7 8 9
While watching TV	Yes	No	1 2 3 4 5 6 7 8 9
When visitors are in your home	Yes	No	1 2 3 4 5 6 7 8 9
When you are visiting someone else	Yes	No	1 2 3 4 5 6 7 8 9
At church or Sunday school	Yes	No	1 2 3 4 5 6 7 8 9
In supermarkets, stores, restaurants, or other public areas	Yes	No	1 2 3 4 5 6 7 8 9
When asked to do chores at home	Yes	No	1 2 3 4 5 6 7 8 9
During conversations with others	Yes	No	1 2 3 4 5 6 7 8 9
While in the car	Yes	No	1 2 3 4 5 6 7 8 9
When father is home	Yes	No	1 2 3 4 5 6 7 8 9
When asked to do school homework	Yes	No	1 2 3 4 5 6 7 8 9

Office Use Only: No. of problems _____ Mean severity _____

Note. From *The Home and School Situations Questionnaires—Revised: Normative Data, Reliability, and Validity* by G. J. DuPaul, 1990, unpublished manuscript, University of Massachusetts Medical Center, Worcester. Reprinted by permission of the author. This form may be reproduced for personal use.

SCHOOL SITUATIONS QUESTIONNAIRE—REVISED

Name of Child _____

Name of Person Completing This Form _____

Does this child have problems paying attention or concentrating in any of these situations? If so, indicate how severe these attentional difficulties are.

Situations	*Yes/No* (Circle one)		*If yes, how severe?* Mild (Circle one) Severe
During individual deskwork	Yes	No	1 2 3 4 5 6 7 8 9
During small-group activities	Yes	No	1 2 3 4 5 6 7 8 9
During free-play time in class	Yes	No	1 2 3 4 5 6 7 8 9
During lectures to the class	Yes	No	1 2 3 4 5 6 7 8 9
On field trips	Yes	No	1 2 3 4 5 6 7 8 9
During special assemblies	Yes	No	1 2 3 4 5 6 7 8 9
During movies, filmstrips	Yes	No	1 2 3 4 5 6 7 8 9
During class discussions	Yes	No	1 2 3 4 5 6 7 8 9

Office Use Only: No. problems _____ Mean severity _____

Note. From *The Home and School Situations Questionnaires—Revised: Normative Data, Reliability, and Validity* by G. J. DuPaul, 1990, unpublished manuscript, University of Massachusetts Medical Center, Worcester. Reprinted by permission of the author. This form may be reproduced for personal use.

MEANS AND STANDARD DEVIATIONS FOR THE HSQ-R BY AGE AND GENDER

Age	Number of problem settings	Mean severity	Factor I	Factor II
	Girls			
6 (*n* = 45)				
M	4.49	3.02	11.62	6.33
SD	3.82	1.88	15.02	9.19
7 (*n* = 70)				
M	4.37	3.13	13.11	5.75
SD	4.13	1.75	16.74	9.86
8 (*n* = 51)				
M	4.39	3.08	13.25	6.33
SD	3.82	1.67	16.28	10.97
9 (*n* = 52)				
M	4.62	3.16	13.58	8.45
SD	4.41	1.81	17.21	13.87
10 (*n* = 45)				
M	3.56	2.99	11.87	5.74
SD	4.19	1.79	18.40	10.96
11 (*n* = 34)				
M	2.03	3.40	6.15	3.46
SD	2.71	2.16	10.52	6.68
12 (*n* = 21)				
M	3.19	3.15	11.43	6.00
SD	4.11	2.08	18.78	14.40
	Boys			
6 (*n* = 54)				
M	5.44	3.39	17.46	9.10
SD	3.60	1.81	17.94	13.41
7 (*n* = 42)				
M	3.76	3.09	13.46	7.96
SD	4.32	1.89	21.00	14.58
8 (*n* = 37)				
M	5.19	3.61	18.43	11.36
SD	4.50	1.85	20.97	15.45
9 (*n* = 33)				
M	4.42	3.69	15.68	7.91
SD	4.12	1.95	18.20	12.31
10 (*n* = 41)				
M	5.15	3.17	14.95	8.78
SD	4.64	1.84	17.54	11.40
11 (*n* = 36)				
M	4.67	3.05	13.22	8.82
SD	4.70	1.80	17.76	14.89

Age	Number of problem settings	Mean severity	Factor I	Factor II
		Boys		
12 (*n* = 20)				
M	4.00	3.86	17.29	5.41
SD	3.23	1.84	18.37	8.47

Note. From *The Home and School Situations Questionnaires—Revised: Normative Data, Reliability, and Validity* by G. J. DuPaul, 1990, unpublished manuscript, University of Massachusetts Medical Center, Worcester. Reprinted by permission of the author.

MEANS AND STANDARD DEVIATIONS FOR THE SSQ-R BY GENDER AND AGE

	Girls		Boys	
Age	Number of problem settings	Mean severity	Number of problem settings	Mean severity
6 (*n* = 42)				
M	2.84	3.47	2.12	4.82
SD	3.26	2.01	3.10	2.30
7 (*n* = 78)				
M	2.40	3.50	3.30	3.85
SD	2.94	1.91	3.17	2.00
8 (*n* = 90)				
M	2.12	3.02	2.50	3.14
SD	2.59	1.36	2.80	1.41
9 (*n* = 78)				
M	2.79	3.81	3.49	4.23
SD	3.13	1.72	3.38	1.98
10 (*n* = 78)				
M	2.32	3.18	2.98	3.56
SD	2.80	1.93	3.08	1.68
11 (*n* = 88)				
M	2.00	2.99	3.86	4.01
SD	2.62	2.00	3.11	2.56
12 (*n* = 36)				
M	2.06	3.01	3.70	3.37
SD	2.64	2.03	2.94	2.01

Note. From *The Home and School Situations Questionnaires—Revised: Normative Data, Reliability, and Validity* by G. J. DuPaul, 1990, unpublished manuscript, University of Massachusetts Medical Center, Worcester. Reprinted by permission of the author.

Academic Performance Rating Scale

This scale was developed by my colleague, Dr. George DuPaul, to assess children's productivity and accuracy in completing school work. It also contains questions that deal with organization and attention skills. Score the scale according to the instructions below and then compare the child's scores to those in the table of norms. Scores greater than 1.5 standard deviations from the mean (93rd%) are considered clinically significant.

ACADEMIC PERFORMANCE RATING SCALE

Student _____ **Date** _____

Age _____   **Grade** _____ **Teacher** _____

For each of the below items, please estimate the above student's performance over the *past week*. For each item, please circle *one* choice only.

1. Estimate the percentage of written math work *completed* (regardless of accuracy) relative to classmates.	0–49% 1	50–69% 2	70–79% 3	80–89% 4	90–100% 5
2. Estimate the percentage of written language arts work *completed* (regardless of accuracy) relative to classmates.	0–49% 1	50–69% 2	70–79% 3	80–89% 4	90–100% 5
3. Estimate the *accuracy* of completed written math work (i.e., percent correct of work done).	0–64% 1	65–69% 2	70–79% 3	80–89% 4	90–100% 5
4. Estimate the *accuracy* of completed written language arts work (i.e., percent correct of work done).	0–64% 1	65–69% 2	70–79% 3	80–89% 4	90–100% 5
5. How consistent has the quality of this child's academic work been over the past week?	Consistently poor 1	More poor than successful 2	Variable 3	More successful than poor 4	Consistently successful 5
6. How frequently does the student accurately follow teacher instructions and/or class discussion during *large-group* (e.g., whole class) instruction?	Never 1	Rarely 2	Sometimes 3	Often 4	Very often 5
7. How frequently does the student accurately follow teacher instructions and/or class discussion during *small-group* (e.g., reading group) instruction?	Never 1	Rarely 2	Sometimes 3	Often 4	Very often 5
8. How quickly does this child learn new material (i.e., pick up novel concepts)?	Very slowly 1	Slowly 2	Average 3	Quickly 4	Very quickly 5

9. What is the quality or neatness of this child's handwriting?	Poor	Fair	Average	Above average	Excellent
	1	2	3	4	5
10. What is the quality of this child's reading skills?	Poor	Fair	Average	Above average	Excellent
	1	2	3	4	5
11. What is the quality of this child's speaking skills?	Poor	Fair	Average	Above average	Excellent
	1	2	3	4	5
12. How often does the child complete written work in a careless, hasty fashion?	Never	Rarely	Sometimes	Often	Very often
	1	2	3	4	5
13. How frequently does the child take more time to complete work than his/her classmates?	Never	Rarely	Sometimes	Often	Very often
	1	2	3	4	5
14. How often is the child able to pay attention without you prompting him/her?	Never	Rarely	Sometimes	Often	Very often
	1	2	3	4	5
15. How frequently does this child require your assistance to accurately complete his/her academic work?	Never	Rarely	Sometimes	Often	Very often
	1	2	3	4	5
16. How often does the child begin written work prior to understanding the directions?	Never	Rarely	Sometimes	Often	Very often
	1	2	3	4	5
17. How frequently does this child have difficulty recalling material from a previous day's lessons?	Never	Rarely	Sometimes	Often	Very often
	1	2	3	4	5
18. How often does the child appear to be staring excessively or "spaced out"?	Never	Rarely	Sometimes	Often	Very often
	1	2	3	4	5
19. How often does the child appear withdrawn or tend to lack an emotional response in a social situation?	Never	Rarely	Sometimes	Often	Very often
	1	2	3	4	5

Note. From *Teacher Ratings of Academic Performance: The Development of the Academic Performance Rating Scale* by G. J. DuPaul, M. Rapport, and L. M. Perriello, 1990, unpublished manuscript, University of Massachusetts Medical Center, Worcester. Reprinted by permission of the authors. This form may be reproduced for personal use.

SCORING INSTRUCTIONS: ACADEMIC PERFORMANCE RATING SCALE

Total score: Sum items 1–19 with the following items reverse-keyed: 12, 13, 15, 16, 17, 18, 19.

Learning Ability: Sum items 3–5, 8, 10, 11, 15, 17 with items 15 & 17 reverse-keyed.

Impulse Control: Sum items 6, 7, 9, 12, 14, 16 with items 12 & 16 reverse-keyed.

Academic Performance: Sum items 1–7, 13, 14 with item 13 reverse-keyed.

Social Withdrawal: Sum items 13, 15, 17–19 with all items reverse-keyed.

MEANS AND STANDARD DEVIATIONS FOR THE ACADEMIC PERFORMANCE RATING SCALE BY GRADE AND GENDER

Grade	Total score	Learning Ability	Impulse Control	Academic Performance	Social Withdrawal
			Girls		
Grade 1 (*n* = 40)					
M	67.02	27.15	21.05	33.98	16.83
SD	16.27	8.41	4.46	8.49	4.83
Grade 2 (*n* = 45)					
M	72.56	29.89	22.59	36.46	18.26
SD	12.33	6.44	3.91	6.22	4.37
Grade 3 (*n* = 42)					
M	72.10	28.62	23.00	35.93	18.77
SD	14.43	6.85	4.92	7.34	3.82
Grade 4 (*n* = 38)					
M	67.79	27.29	22.15	33.32	17.41
SD	18.69	8.57	5.27	9.28	5.08
Grade 5 (*n* = 44)					
M	73.02	29.39	23.58	37.00	18.31
SD	14.10	6.90	4.07	6.43	4.44
Grade 6 (*n* = 31)					
M	74.10	30.13	23.00	36.74	19.17
SD	14.45	7.28	4.31	7.09	3.71
			Boys		
Grade 1 (*n* = 42)					
M	71.95	30.19	22.86	35.52	17.88
SD	16.09	7.22	5.02	8.85	4.50
Grade 2 (*n* = 44)					
M	67.84	28.44	20.79	33.80	16.64
SD	14.86	7.11	4.59	8.43	5.10
Grade 3 (*n* = 49)					
M	68.49	28.39	20.90	34.71	17.67
SD	16.96	7.31	5.47	9.08	4.73
Grade 4 (*n* = 40)					
M	69.77	28.50	21.78	34.36	18.40
SD	15.83	7.51	4.90	8.40	4.21

Grade	Total score	Learning Ability	Impulse Control	Academic Performance	Social Withdrawal
			Boys		
Grade 5 ($n=34$)					
M	63.68	26.00	19.86	32.09	16.56
SD	18.04	8.15	5.17	9.83	5.15
Grade 6 ($n=38$)					
M	65.24	26.64	20.08	33.22	16.78
SD	12.39	6.52	3.86	6.39	4.05

Note. From *Teacher Ratings of Academic Performance: The Development of the Academic Performance Rating Scale* by G. J. DuPaul, M. Rapport, and L. M. Perriello, 1990, unpublished manuscript, University of Massachusetts Medical Center, Worcester. Reprinted by permission of the authors.

Children's Atypical Development Scale

My colleagues David Guevremont, Ph.D., and David Dinklage, Ph.D., developed this scale as a means of assessing clinically significant symptoms of thought disturbance or affective disorders in clinic-referred children. The Children's Atypical Development Scale (CADS) has not been used with a normal population to determine the frequency with which these items occur in normal children or to evaluate the factor structure of the scale. However, we would not antic-ipate finding many of these items in normal children given their severity and the fact that they were chosen precisely because they were so atypical of normal children. The table that follows the scale illustrates the frequency with which these items were endorsed in a group of ADHD children compared with children having significant affective or thought disorders (Multiplex Developmental Disorder or Atypical Pervasive Developmental Disorder).

CHILDREN'S ATYPICAL DEVELOPMENT SCALE (CADS)

Child's name: _____ **Sex:** M   F

Race: _____   **Date of birth:** _____

This form was filled out by: _____

Below is a list of behaviors. For each item, please circle 2 if the item is very true or often true of your child. Circle 1 if the item is somewhat or sometimes true. If the item is not true of your child, circle 0. Please answer all items as well as you can, even if some do not seem to apply to your child.

0 = NOT TRUE	1 = SOMEWHAT OR SOMETIMES TRUE	2 = VERY TRUE OR OFTEN TRUE

0   1   2   1. "Misses the point" or main idea in conversation

0   1   2   2. Rambling speech—one idea is not connected to the next

0   1   2   3. Refers to self in the third person (e.g., uses own name instead of "I" or "me")

0   1   2   4. Makes odd noises/talks in odd voices

0   1   2   5. Obsessive interest in narrow or atypical topic or event (e.g., death, the supernatural, anatomy, fantasy characters)

0   1   2   6. Makes irrelevant comments

0   1   2   7. Insists on sticking to unusual routines

0   1   2   8. Lacks interest in toys or uses toys in an unusual manner

0   1   2   9. Strong attachments to inanimate objects

0   1   2   10. Unusual aversions to neutral objects or situations (e.g., will not wear certain materials, refuses to walk up a certain stairway)

0   1   2   11. Engages in repetitive or stereotypic behavior (e.g., shakes or flaps hands, repeatedly touches hair or other material)

0   1   2   12. Extreme reactions to minor inconveniences or irritations

0   1   2   13. Difficulties dealing with change in daily schedule or routines

0   1   2   14. Marked lack of concern for appearance

0   1   2   15. Lacks social discretion (e.g., comments on people's behavior in public without concern for their reaction or feelings)

0   1   2   16. Acts as if other people were not in the same room

0   1   2   17. Poor judge of other people's reactions or feelings

0   1   2   18. Reveals overly personal detail to acquaintances or strangers

0   1   2   19. Lacks interest in peers

0   1   2   20. Makes poor eye contact with others

0   1   2   21. Does not appreciate personal space (e.g., stands too close or talks with back to person)

0   1   2   22. Mood changes quickly without apparent reason

0   1   2   23. Describes the details of an event but misses the meaning or importance of it

0   1   2   24. Sits, stands, or walks in odd postures

0   1   2   25. Attributes meaning to events that are simply a coincidence

0   1   2   26. Believes others are talking about him/her when others are speaking softly among themselves

0	1	2	27. Overly suspicious of others
0	1	2	28. Confuses the sequence in which events occurred when describing them
0	1	2	29. Lacks compassion when others are hurt or finds it humorous
0	1	2	30. Laughs or cries for little apparent reason
0	1	2	31. Attends to background or distant sound that others would ignore
0	1	2	32. Excessively preoccupied with violent stories, TV shows, or weapons
0	1	2	33. Confuses the causes of events or fails to understand how events cause other events
0	1	2	34. Draws excessively detailed pictures
0	1	2	35. Dislikes being held or touched
0	1	2	36. Keeps a diary or journal of rambling thoughts or random ideas
0	1	2	37. Speaks in half-thoughts or incomplete phrases without concern for whether others can understand or follow his/her ideas
0	1	2	38. Gets angry for little apparent reason
0	1	2	39. Has unusual fears not typical for his/her age group (e.g., afraid to take shower or put head under the water after 6 years of age)
0	1	2	40. Hoards worthless objects that have no apparent meaning or value
0	1	2	41. Speaks in excessively loud or soft voices
0	1	2	42. Overreacts to pain (e.g., bumps leg and screams or cries excessively)
0	1	2	43. Exhibits ritualistic behavior (e.g., has to line up toys in a particular order after using them)
0	1	2	44. Spends an unusual amount of time fantasizing
0	1	2	45. Mouths or chews objects
0	1	2	46. Seems to be extremely naive for his/her age (e.g., believes anything he/she is told)
0	1	2	47. Does not respond to the initiations of other children
0	1	2	48. Picks nose, skin, or other parts of the body
0	1	2	49. Makes bizarre statements
0	1	2	50. Interacts with acquaintances and strangers in a similar manner
0	1	2	51. Hits or bites self
0	1	2	52. Repeats certain acts over and over
0	1	2	53. Lacks modesty for his/her age

Note. Reprinted by permission of the developers, David Guevremont and David Dinklage. This form may be reproduced for personal use.

RESULTS OF A PILOT STUDY TO DEVELOP A RATING SCALE FOR MULTIPLEX DEVELOPMENTAL DISORDER

1. Misses the point or main idea in a conversation (43 vs. 15%)
2. Rambling speech—one idea is not connected to the next (35 vs. 5%)
6. Makes irrelevant comments (48 vs. 10%)
7. *Insists on sticking to unusual routines (57 vs. 0%)*
9. Strong attachments to inanimate objects (43 vs. 5%)
11. *Engages in repetitive or stereotypic behavior (e.g., shakes or flaps hands, repeatedly touches hair or other material) (65 vs. 0%)*
12. *Extreme reactions to minor inconveniences or irritations (65 vs. 30%)*
13. *Difficulties dealing with change in daily schedule or routines (61 vs. 15%)*
14. Marked lack of concern for appearance (43 vs. 15%)
15. *Lacks social discretion (e.g., comments on people's behavior in public without concern for their reaction or feelings) (65 vs. 10%)*
17. *Poor judge of other people's reactions or feelings (61 vs. 15%)*
19. Lacks interest in peers (39 vs. 5%)
20. Makes poor eye contact with others (39 vs. 5%)
22. *Mood changes quickly without apparent reason (55 vs. 30%)*
23. Describes the details of an event but misses the meaning or importance of it (39 vs. 5%)
29. Lacks compassion when others are hurt or finds it humorous (39 vs. 0%)
30. *Laughs or cries for little apparent reason (57 vs. 20%)*
31. *Attends to background or distant sound that others would ignore (57 vs. 5%)*
33. *Confuses the causes of events or fails to understand how events cause other events (61 vs. 10%)*
37. Speaks in half-thoughts or incomplete phrases without concern for whether others can understand or follow his/her thoughts (35 vs. 5%)
38. Gets angry for little apparent reason (48 vs. 30%)
39. Has unusual fears not typical for his/her age group (e.g., afraid to take a shower or put head under the water after 6 years of age) (35 vs. 5%)
40. Hoards worthless objects that have no apparent meaning or value (35 vs. 10%)
41. Speaks in excessively loud or soft voices (48 vs. 25%)
44. Spends an unusual amount of time fantasizing (35 vs. 5%)
46. *Seems to be extremely naive for his/her age (e.g., believes anything he/she is told) (57 vs. 10%)*
48. Picks nose, skin, or other parts of the body (48 vs. 20%)
49. Makes bizarre statements (35 vs. 10%)
52. Repeats certain acts over and over (35 vs. 5%)
53. Lacks modesty for his/her age (48 vs. 10%)

Note. The percentages given here indicate the proportion of parents in the MDD and ADHD groups, respectively, who endorsed these items. Items were included in the table if they were endorsed by at least 35 percent of the MDD parents; items endorsed by more than 50 percent of these are italicized. Results are reprinted with permission of David Guevremont and David Dinklage, the principal investigators in this study.

Observation Form for Recording ADHD Behaviors During Academic Performance in the Clinic or in School

CONDUCTING THE BEHAVIORAL OBSERVATIONS DURING THE RESTRICTED ACADEMIC SITUATION

This task is designed to observe and record symptoms of ADHD during individual academic work, such as that which might be given as homework or in-class deskwork to a child. The task involves the following procedures:

In-Clinic Observations

1. Place the child in a playroom containing toys, a small work table and chair, a one-way mirror, and an intercom. Let the child play for 5 minutes as a habituation period.

2. Enter the room and tell the child that you now have some schoolwork for him or her to do. Tell the child to sit at the small table, stay in the chair, and complete the packet of math problems. Tell the child not to play with any toys and not to leave the seat during this work time; you will be back in a while to see how much work he or she has done. Be sure to give the child a set of math problems at a difficulty level well below the child's current grade. We typically use a set that is one grade level below that grade in which the child is currently placed.

3. Leave the playroom, enter the observation room, and begin coding the child's behavior using

the procedures described below. After 15 to 20 minutes, end the coding session.

In-School Observations

Observe the child in his or her regular classroom for 15 to 20 minutes when the child has been given academic work to do alone at his or her desk. You can either have the teacher give work that is from a current assignment or take in a set of math problems you have specially constructed for this exercise. In any case, be sure the child has been given enough work to occupy 15 to 20 minutes. Have the teacher tell the child to go to his or her desk, complete the assigned packet of work, and stay in the seat. Then begin to observe and record the child, using the procedures below.

For a normative comparison, ask the teacher to point out an average child in that classroom and code that child's behavior during individual deskwork for the same period of time.

To increase the validity of your school observations, take several observations over several days to increase the sampling of child behavior.

Coding Instructions

It is helpful to make a tape recording that contains cues for the beginning of each 30-second interval of observation. This tape can simply say, "Begin 1" and then 30 seconds later "Begin 2," and so on for the 30 observation intervals. We use 30-second intervals over a 15-minute observation period, but others have used 15- or 20-second coding intervals over 20 minutes or more of observation to increase the sensitivity of the measure. When the tape sounds the beginning of a coding interval, observe the child and place a check mark next to any of the behavior categories that occur, using the column marked for that coding interval (1, 2, 3, . . .). When the next interval begins, move to the next column and again place a check beside any of the behavior categories that occur. Once a behavior has been checked during an interval, it cannot be checked again until the next interval.

At the end of the observation period, calculate the percentage occurrence of each behavior category by dividing the number of check marks for that category by the total number of recording intervals. You should also calculate the number of math problems completed and the percentage completed correctly.

Definitions

1. *Off task:* This category is checked if the child interrupts his or her attention to the tasks to engage in some other behavior. Attention is defined as visually looking at the task materials. If the child breaks eye contact with the math problems, then he or she is coded as off task.

2. *Fidgeting:* Any repetitive, purposeless motion of the legs, arms, hands, buttocks, or trunk. It must occur at least twice in succession to be considered repetitive, and it should serve no purpose. Examples include swaying back and forth, kicking one's legs back and forth, swinging arms at one's side, shuffling feet from side to side, shifting one's buttocks about in the chair, tapping a pencil or finger repeatedly on the table, and so on.

3. *Vocalizing:* Any vocal noise or verbalization made by the child. Examples: speech, whispering, singing, humming, making odd mouth noises, clicking one's teeth, and so on.

4. *Plays with objects:* Touching any object in the room besides the table, chair, math problems, and pencil. The child may touch his or her own clothing without being considered to play with an object. However, touching toys, walls, light switches, curtains, or any other object in the room is coded in this category.

5. *Out of seat:* Any time the child's buttocks break contact with the flat surface of the seat.

RESTRICTED ACADEMIC SITUATION CODING SHEET

Interval #:	1	2	3	4	5	6	7	8	9	10	11	12	13	14	15
Off task															
Fidgeting															
Vocalizing															
Plays w/obj.															
Out of seat															

Interval #:	16	17	18	19	20	21	22	23	24	25	26	27	28	29	30
Off task															
Fidgeting															
Vocalizing															
Plays w/obj.															
Out of seat															

Interval #:	31	32	33	34	35	36	37	38	39	40	Total
Off task											/40
Fidgeting											/40
Vocalizing											/40
Plays w/obj.											/40
Out of seat											/40

Total: /200

Child's Name: _____

Coder Initials: _____

Date: _____

Week #   Initial   Wk 1   Wk 2   Wk 3   Wk 4

Comments:

Issues Checklist for Parents and Teenagers

This scale was developed by Arthur Robin, Ph.D., and Sharon Foster, Ph.D., to assess the intensity of conflicts that adolescents have with their parents. Such information is very helpful in tailoring a family therapy program to the needs of a particular family and in monitoring the effectiveness of therapy. The scoring instructions and norms are contained in the following pages.

Deviant scores are considered to be 1.5 to 2 standard deviations above the mean. However, even if the scores are not deviant, parents and teens may still be sufficiently concerned about particular communication problems and conflicts to require some type of intervention.

For a treatment approach, I recommend the Robin and Foster treatment program for parent–adolescent conflicts entitled *Problem Solving—Communication Training*. It can be obtained in their book, *Negotiating Parent–Adolescent Conflict* available from the Guilford Press, New York. The program by Gerald Patterson and Marion Forgatch, *Parents and Adolescents Living Together* (Castalia Press, Eugene, Ore.) is similar and also excellent.

* * *

DESCRIPTION

The issues Checklist (IC) assesses self-reports of specific disputes between parents and teenagers (Prinz, Foster, Kent, & O'Leary, 1979). It consists of a list of 44 issues that can lead to disagreements between parents and adolescents, such as chores, curfew, bedtime, friends, and homework. Parents and adolescents complete identical versions of the IC. Adolescents in two-parent families complete it separately for disputes with their mothers and fathers.

For each topic, the respondent indicates whether the issue has been broached during the previous 4 weeks. For each topic reported as having been discussed the respondent rates the affectual intensity of the discussions on a 5-point scale ranging from calm to angry and estimates how often the topics come up. The IC yields three scores for each respondent: (1) the quantity of issues (the total number of issues checked as broached); (2) the anger-intensity of issues (an average of the anger-intensity ratings for all of the endorsed issues); and (3) the weighted average of the frequency and anger-intensity level of issues (a score obtained by multiplying each frequency estimate by its associated intensity, summing these cross products, then dividing by the total of all the frequency estimates). The weighted average provides an estimate of the anger *per discussion*, whereas the intensity score reflects the average anger *per issue*, regardless of the frequency with which the issue was discussed.

PURPOSE

The IC is designed to provide scientific information regarding the frequency and content of disputes between parents and adolescents and the perceived anger-intensity level of these disputes. It covers a

Note. From *Dictionary of Behavioral Assessment* (pp. 278–279), M. Hersen & A. S. Bellack, Eds., New York, Pergamon Press, 1988. Copyright 1988 by Pergamon Press. Reprinted by permission of the publisher.

broad array of possible disputes applicable to 12–16-year-old teenagers and their parents.

DEVELOPMENT

The IC was constructed by revising a similar instrument developed by the first author, with issues selected based upon literature on parent–adolescent relationships and clinical experience. No pilot testing was done prior to formal validation studies.

PSYCHOMETRIC CHARACTERISTICS

The reliability, discriminant/criterion-related validity, and treatment sensitivity of the IC has been examined in a number of investigations. Estimates of test–retest reliability were computed in two studies. Using small sample data collected over 6–8-week intervals from the waitlist groups of two outcome studies (Foster, Prinz, & O'Leary, 1983; Robin, 1981), adolescent reliability ranged from .49 to .87 for the quantity of issues, .37 to .49 for the anger-intensity score, and .15 to .24 for the weighted frequency by intensity score. Parental reliability was higher, averaging .65 and .55 for mother and father quantity of issues, .81 and .66 for mother and father anger-intensity scores, and .90 and .40 for mother and father weighted frequency by anger-intensity scores. Using 33 nonclinic families assessed over 1–2-week intervals, Enyart (1984) found somewhat higher reliabilities, particularly for adolescents (range = .49–.80).

Agreement reliability between mothers and adolescents, assessed by examining whether parents and adolescents concurred that an issue either had or had not been discussed, averaged 68% (range = 38%–86%). When the congruence of mother and adolescent responses was examined via correlations, results ranged from .10 to .64 (mean $r = .28$). These results raise questions about the accuracy of the IC as a measure of actual discussions at home.

The discriminant/criterion-related validity of the IC has been studied by contrasting the responses of distressed parents and adolescents (referred for treatment of family relationship problems) with the responses of nondistressed parents and teenagers (no history of treatment and self-reports of satisfactory relationships). Aggregated data from three assess-ment and two treatment studies with adolescents aged 10–18, male and female, revealed that all of the IC scores discriminated between groups, with the most pronounced effects on maternal anger-intensity scores (accounting for 48% of the variance in distress/nondistressed status) and paternal quantity of issues scores (36% of the variance) (Robin & Foster, 1984). Adolescent effects were much weaker, explaining 3%–19% of the variance (mean = 12%). Across all scores, distressed family members reported significantly more frequent, angrier disputes than nondistressed family members.

When the IC was used as a pre–post measure of change, treatment outcome studies of both a problem-solving communication skill training program and a heterogeneous nonbehavioral family therapy revealed significant decrements in anger-intensity and weighted frequency by anger-intensity scores following intervention (Foster et al., 1983; Robin, 1981)

CLINICAL USE

The clinician can use the IC to pinpoint sources of conflict and survey which topics are perceived as provoking the greatest amounts of anger. These topics ordinarily are selected by family members as their most important problems and often warrant further assessment via interviews and/or home data collection. Ratings of IC issues can also help the therapist sequence a skill-oriented treatment so that early intervention sessions focus on less intense conflicts and later sessions address more intense problems. Noting discrepancies between parent and adolescent ICs and inquiring further about them can also yield invaluable information about differential perceptions within the family system. Preliminary norms from distressed and nondistressed families are also available (Robin & Foster, 1984). Since the IC was validated on families with adolescents experiencing externalizing behavior disorders (Attention Deficit Disorder, Conduct Disorder, etc.), its psychometric properties with families in which the adolescents have other presenting problems are unknown. Thus, it should be interpreted cautiously with such populations.

FUTURE DIRECTIONS

The most important unanswered question concerning the IC is the extent to which reports of specific disputes correspond to actual disputes. The low reliability suggests that the IC may not be an accurate measure of actual interactions. Correlational studies comparing retrospective IC scores to daily reports and direct observations of family disputes are needed. In addition, a broader-based normative sample including distressed families with a variety of presenting problems would be desirable.

REFERENCES

Enyart, P. (1984). *Behavioral correlates of self-reported parent-adolescent relationship satisfaction.* Unpublished doctoral dissertation, West Virginia University, Morgantown.

Foster, S. L., Prinz, R. J., & O'Leary, K. D. (1983). Impact of problem-solving communication training and generalization procedures on family conflict. *Child and Family Behavior Therapy, 5,* 1–23.

Prinz, R. J., Foster, S. L., Kent, R. N., & O'Leary, K. D. (1983). Multivariate assessment of conflict in distressed and nondistressed mother–adolescent dyads. *Journal of Applied Behavior Analysis, 12,* 691–700.

Robin, A. L. (1981). A controlled evaluation of problem-solving communication training with parent–adolescent conflict. *Behavior Therapy, 12,* 593–609.

Robin, A. L., & Foster, S. L. (1984). Problem solving communication training: A behavioral-family systems approach to parent–adolescent conflict. In P. Karoly and J. J. Steffen (Eds.), *Adolescent behavior disorders: Foundations and contemporary concerns* (pp. 195–240). Lexington, MA: D.C. Heath.

ISSUES CHECKLIST

Name: _____ **Date:** _____

☐ Adolescent   ☐ Adolescent
☐ Mother   *with*   ☐ Mother
☐ Father   ☐ Father

Below is a list of things that sometimes get talked about at home. We would like you to look carefully at each topic on the left-hand side of the page and decide whether the *two of you together* have talked about that topic *at all* during the last 2 weeks.

If the two of you together have discussed it during the last 2 weeks, circle *Yes* to the right of the topic.

If the two of you together have *not* discussed it during the last 2 weeks, circle *No* to the right of the topic.

Now, we would like you to go back over the list of topics. For those topics for which you circled *Yes*, please answer the two questions on the right-hand side of the page.

1. How many times during the last 2 weeks did the topic come up?

2. How hot are the discussions?

Go down this column for all pages.   Go down this column for all pages.

Topic			How many times?	How hot are the discussions?					
				Calm		A little angry		Angry	
1. Telephone calls	Yes	No		1	2	3	4	5	
2. Time for going to bed	Yes	No		1	2	3	4	5	
3. Cleaning up bedroom	Yes	No		1	2	3	4	5	
4. Doing homework	Yes	No		1	2	3	4	5	
5. Putting away clothes	Yes	No		1	2	3	4	5	
6. Using the television	Yes	No		1	2	3	4	5	
7. Cleanliness (washing, showers, brushing teeth)	Yes	No		1	2	3	4	5	
8. Which clothes to wear	Yes	No		1	2	3	4	5	
9. How neat clothing looks	Yes	No		1	2	3	4	5	
10. Making too much noise at home	Yes	No		1	2	3	4	5	
11. Table manners	Yes	No		1	2	3	4	5	
12. Fighting with brothers or sisters	Yes	No		1	2	3	4	5	
13. Cursing	Yes	No		1	2	3	4	5	
14. How money is spent	Yes	No		1	2	3	4	5	

Topic			How many times?	How hot are the discussions?				
				Calm		A little angry		Angry
15. Picking books or movies	Yes	No		1	2	3	4	5
16. Allowance	Yes	No		1	2	3	4	5
17. Going places without parents (shopping, movies, etc.)	Yes	No		1	2	3	4	5
18. Playing stereo or radio too loudly	Yes	No		1	2	3	4	5
19. Turning off lights in house	Yes	No		1	2	3	4	5
20. Drugs	Yes	No		1	2	3	4	5
21. Taking care of records, games, toys, and things	Yes	No		1	2	3	4	5
22. Drinking beer or other liquor	Yes	No		1	2	3	4	5
23. Buying records, games, toys, and things	Yes	No		1	2	3	4	5
24. Going on dates	Yes	No		1	2	3	4	5
25. Who should be friends	Yes	No		1	2	3	4	5
26. Selecting new clothing	Yes	No		1	2	3	4	5
27. Sex	Yes	No		1	2	3	4	5
28. Coming home on time	Yes	No		1	2	3	4	5
29. Getting to school on time	Yes	No		1	2	3	4	5
30. Getting low grades in school	Yes	No		1	2	3	4	5
31. Getting in trouble in school	Yes	No		1	2	3	4	5
32. Lying	Yes	No		1	2	3	4	5
33. Helping out around the house	Yes	No		1	2	3	4	5
34. Talking back to parents	Yes	No		1	2	3	4	5
35. Getting up in the morning	Yes	No		1	2	3	4	5
36. Bothering parents when they want to be left alone	Yes	No		1	2	3	4	5
37. Bothering teenager when he/she wants to be left alone	Yes	No		1	2	3	4	5
38. Putting feet on furniture	Yes	No		1	2	3	4	5
39. Messing up the house	Yes	No		1	2	3	4	5
40. What time to have meals	Yes	No		1	2	3	4	5
41. How to spend free time	Yes	No		1	2	3	4	5

Topic			How many times?	How hot are the discussions?				
				Calm		A little angry		Angry
42. Smoking	Yes	No		1	2	3	4	5
43. Earning money away from house	Yes	No		1	2	3	4	5
44. What teenager eats	Yes	No		1	2	3	4	5

Check to see that you circled Yes or No for every topic. Then tell the interviewer you are finished.

Tell interviewer you are finished.

Note. From *Negotiating Parent-Adolescent Conflict* by A. L. Robin and S. L. Foster, 1989, New York: Guilford Press. Copyright 1989 by The Guilford Press. Reprinted by permission of the authors and publisher.

SCORING INSTRUCTIONS: ISSUES CHECKLIST

This is a measure of the frequency and anger-intensity level of specific disputes between parents and teenagers. Three scores are computed as indicated below, and the results can be compared to normative data to make inferences about the level of specific disputes for a given family.

1. *Quantity of issue.* Sum the number of issues checked Yes.
2. *Anger-intensity level of issues.* For issues checked Yes, sum the intensity ratings and divide by the number of issues checked Yes to obtain a mean anger-intensity score.
3. *Weighted frequency by anger-intensity level of issues.*
   a. Multiply each frequency by its associated anger-intensity score.
   b. Sum the products of each intensity times frequency.
   c. Sum the frequencies.
   d. Divide the sum of the products by the sum of the frequencies.

NORMS FOR THE ISSUES CHECKLIST

	Distressed			Nondistressed				
	n	$\bar{x}$	SD	n	$\bar{x}$	SD	t	r_{pbs}[a]
Maternal quantity	124	22.55	7.35	68	17.83	7.07	3.62**	.25
Maternal anger intensity	124	2.42	0.46	68	1.70	0.45	11.43**	.64
Maternal anger intensity × frequency	124	2.29	2.15	68	0.83	1.08	5.21**	.35
Adolescent-mother quantity	96	20.68	7.59	68	18.46	7.25	1.88*	.15
Adolescent-mother anger intensity	96	2.34	0.63	68	1.77	0.49	6.20**	.44
Adolescent-mother anger intensity × frequency	96	1.93	1.81	68	0.84	0.86	4.60**	.40
Paternal quantity	60	18.38	5.05	38	11.64	4.63	6.61**	.60
Paternal anger intensity	60	2.18	0.60	38	1.82	0.57	2.93*	.29
Paternal anger intensity × frequency	60	2.39	0.64	38	1.94	0.59	3.46**	.33
Adolescent-father quantity	38	13.60	5.54	14	10.71	4.65	1.71*	.24
Adolescent-father anger intensity	38	2.40	0.76	14	1.75	0.64	2.80*	.37
Adolescent-father anger intensity × frequency	38	2.72	0.95	14	1.88	0.69	2.97*	.39

Note. From *Negotiating Parent-Adolescent Conflict* by A. L. Robin and S. L. Foster, 1989. New York: Guilford Press. Copyright 1989 by The Guilford Press. Reprinted by permission of the authors and publisher.
[a]r_{pbs} = point-biserial correlation between the particular score and group membership (distressed vs. nondistressed).
 *$p < .05$
**$p < .001$

Conflict Behavior Questionnaire

The Conflict Behavior Questionnaire, created by Arthur Robin and Sharon Foster, can be used to assess patterns of negative communication in parent–adolescent relationships. Scoring instructions and norms are provided here along with details on the psychometric properties of the scale.

DESCRIPTION

The Conflict Behavior Questionnaire (CBQ) is a self-report inventory assessing perceived communication and conflict between parents and adolescents. Parents and adolescents complete parallel versions of the CBQ, rating their interactions over the preceding 2–3 weeks. The parent version contains 75 true/false statements, 53 regarding the parents' appraisal of their adolescent's behavior (e.g., "My child sulks after an argument.") and 22 regarding their perception of their interactions with the adolescent (e.g., "We joke around often."). The adolescent version contains 73 items, 51 regarding the adolescent's appraisal of the parent's behavior (e.g., "My mom doesn't understand me.") and 22 identical to the parent form, tapping the adolescent's perception of interactions with the parent.

Separate scores are obtained for each member's appraisal of (a) the other's behavior and (b) the dyadic interaction. In two-parent families adolescents complete the CBQ separately for relations with the mother and the father. Scoring is readily accomplished by constructing transparent overlays following an item key or using machine-scorable optimal-scanning answer sheets.

PURPOSE

The CBQ gives a broad-based estimate of how much conflict and negative communication parents and adolescents experience in their relationships. Items reflect general arguments, misunderstanding, the inability to resolve disputes, and specific verbal and nonverbal communication deficits.

DEVELOPMENT

The CBQ was developed by Prinz, Foster, Kent, and O'Leary (1979) based upon an item pool initially generated by eighth-grade students, clinical psychologists, and research assistants. A sample of 91 college students and 40 mothers responded to the pilot items based on their recall of earlier parent–adolescent relations. Respondents also rated the overall quality of the relationship they were evaluating, and these ratings were used to split the samples into subgroups indicating generally "good" versus "poor" relationships. Items that discriminated between the groups formed the final version.

Subsequently, a short 20-item form was constructed through item analysis by retaining those items which correlated most highly with the total scores and maximally discriminated distressed from nondistressed families. The short form yields a single summary score which correlates .96 with scores from the longer original CBQ.

PSYCHOMETRIC CHARACTERISTICS (LONG FORM)

The internal consistency of the CBQ, assessed with alpha coefficients, has been found to be .90 and above for mothers and adolescents (Prinz et al., 1979), but has not been examined for fathers. Combined data from waitlist control groups in two outcome studies provided preliminary estimates of test–retest reliability over 6–8-week intervals for small samples. Correlations for maternal appraisal of the adolescent and dyad were .57 and .61 respectively ($n = 19$); and for adolescent appraisal of the father and dyad were .84 and .85 respectively ($n = 15$).

The "interrater reliability" of the CBQ, assessed by computing percentage agreement between parents and adolescents on the 22 identical items, averaged 67% for distressed and 84% for nondistressed dyads, a significant difference.

Three studies found evidence for the discriminant/criterion-related validity of the CBQ by contrasting responses of clinic-referred and nonclinic families with 10–18-year-old male and female adolescents (Prinz et al., 1979; Robin & Foster, 1984; Robin & Weiss, 1980). Clinic-referred mothers, fathers, and adolescents reported significantly more negative appraisals of the other members and of the dyadic relationship, with maternal scores explaining the greatest degree of the variance (48%) in distress status. The data from these studies were pooled with the pre-assessment data from two treatment studies to produce aggregated normative data for 137 clinic-referred and 68 nonclinic families (Robin & Foster, 1984).

The CBQ reports have also shown significant decreases for parent and adolescent scores following both behavioral and nonbehavioral family interventions (Foster, Prinz, & O'Leary, 1983; Robin, 1981). In addition, the CBQ correlates moderately (.52) with problem-solving communication behavior coded from audiotaped interaction tasks and with the Dissatisfaction with Childrearing Scale of the Marital Satisfaction Inventory (.55) (Robin & Foster, 1984), yielding evidence for construct validity.

CLINICAL USE

The CBQ can supplement interview and direct observation data in determining the degree of perceived conflict and negative communication in a parent–adolescent relationship, e.g., how distressed the family is. The short form, which takes approximately 5 minutes to complete, makes an excellent waiting-room screening measure. The clinician can estimate severity of conflict by plotting CBQ scores on T-score profiles, which provide visual/quantitative comparisons with normative data from clinic and nonclinic families. By comparing the relative degrees of conflict within each dyad, the clinician can localize relationship problems and supplement the interview for forming hypotheses about family structure.

The CBQ is appropriate for parents and children aged 10–19. It has been used primarily to screen and quantify overt conflict, disputes, and negative interaction in families with adolescents experiencing externalizing behavior disorders (conduct disorders, attention deficit disorders, delinquency). It was not designed for use with families in which the adolescents are experiencing internalizing behavior disorders, schizophrenia, or mental retardation. When conflict is avoided or denied despite basic disagreements between family members, scores on the CBQ may be artificially low and difficult to differentiate from a nondistressed profile.

FUTURE DIRECTIONS

The correspondence between perceived communication and conflict reported on the CBQ and actual conflict and negative communication assessed through direct observation is unclear. The CBQ correlates moderately with observations of conflict in samples of communication, but further investigations using more naturalistic observational and self-monitoring measures are needed. The discrepancies between different family members' scores on identical items raise additional questions about the accuracy of CBQ reports.

The normative data have been collected primarily with white, middle-class urban and suburban families. Further investigations exploring responses of older adolescents and more heterogeneous racial and ethnic populations are sorely needed.

Finally, the utility of the CBQ in discriminating

between a broader range of family types bears further investigation since research to date has focused on adolescents with externalizing behavior disorders.

REFERENCES

Foster, S. L., Prinz, R. J., & O'Leary, K. D. (1983). Impact of problem-solving communication training and generalization procedures on family conflict. *Child and Family Behavior Therapy, 5,* 1–23.

Prinz, R. J., Foster, S. L., Kent, R. N., & O'Leary, K. D. (1979). Multivariate assessment of conflict in distressed and nondistressed mother–adolescent dyads. *Journal of Applied Behavior Analysis, 12,* 691–700.

Robin, A. L. (1981). A controlled evaluation of problem-solving communication training with parent–adolescent conflict. *Behavior Therapy, 12,* 593–609.

Robin, A. L., & Foster, S. L. (1984). Problem-solving communication training: A behavioral-family systems approach to parent-adolescent conflict. In P. Karoly and J. J. Steffen (Eds.), *Adolescent behavior disorders: Foundations and contemporary concerns* (pp. 195–240). Lexington, MA: D.C. Heath.

Robin, A. L., & Weiss, J. (1980). Criterion-related validity of behavioral and self-report measures of problem-solving communication skills in distressed and nondistressed parent–adolescent dyads. *Behavioral Assessment, 2,* 339–352.

CONFLICT BEHAVIOR QUESTIONNAIRE—PARENT VERSION

Name _____

Date _____

I am the child's ____mother ____father (check one).

I am filling this questionnaire out regarding my ____son ____daughter (check one) who is ____ years old.

Think back over the last two weeks at home. The statements below have to do with you and your child. Read the statement, and then decide if you believe that the statement is true. If it is true, then circle **True,** and if you believe the statement is not true, circle **False.** You must circle either True or False, but never both for the same item. Please answer all items. Answer for yourself, without talking it over with anyone.

True	False	1. My child is easy to get along with.
True	False	2. My child is well behaved in our discussions.
True	False	3. My child is receptive to criticism.
True	False	4. For the most part, my child likes to talk to me.
True	False	5. We almost never seem to agree.
True	False	6. My child usually listens to what I tell him/her.
True	False	7. At least three times a week, we get angry at each other.
True	False	8. My child says I have no consideration of his/her feelings.
True	False	9. My child and I compromise during arguments.
True	False	10. My child often doesn't do what I ask.
True	False	11. The talks we have are frustrating.
True	False	12. My child often seems angry at me.
True	False	13. My child acts impatient when I talk.
True	False	14. In general, I don't think we get along very well.
True	False	15. My child almost never understands my side of an argument.
True	False	16. My child and I have big arguments about little things.
True	False	17. My child is defensive when I talk to him.
True	False	18. My child thinks my opinions don't count.
True	False	19. We argue a lot about rules.
True	False	20. My child tells me he/she thinks I am unfair.

CONFLICT BEHAVIOR QUESTIONNAIRE—ADOLESCENT'S VERSION REGARDING MOTHER

Name _____

Date _____

Think back over the last two weeks at home. The statements below have to do with you and your mother. Read the statement, and then decide if you believe that the statement is true. If it is true, then circle **True,** and if you believe the statement is not true, circle **False.** You must circle either True or False, but never both for the same item. Please answer all items.

True   False   1. My mom doesn't understand me.

True   False   2. My mom and I sometimes end our arguments calmly.

True   False   3. We almost never seem to agree.

True   False   4. I enjoy the talks we have.

True   False   5. When I state my own opinion, she gets upset.

True   False   6. At least three times a week, we get angry at each other.

True   False   7. My mother listens when I need someone to talk to.

True   False   8. My mom is a good friend to me.

True   False   9. My mom says I have no consideration for her.

True   False   10. At least once a day we get angry at each other.

True   False   11. My mother is bossy when we talk.

True   False   12. My mom understands me.

True   False   13. The talks we have are frustrating.

True   False   14. My mom understands my point of view, even when she doesn't agree with me.

True   False   15. My mom seems to be always complaining about me.

True   False   16. In general, I don't think we get along very well.

True   False   17. My mom screams a lot.

True   False   18. My mom puts me down.

True   False   19. If I run into problems, my mom helps me out.

True   False   20. I enjoy spending time with my mother.

CONFLICT BEHAVIOR QUESTIONNAIRE—ADOLESCENT'S VERSION REGARDING FATHER

Name _____

Date _____

Think back over the last two weeks at home. The statements below have to do with you and your father. Read the statement, and then decide if you believe that the statement is true. If it is true, then circle **True,** and if you believe the statement is not true, circle **False.** You must circle either True or False, but never both for the same item. Please answer all items.

True   False   1. My dad doesn't understand me.

True   False   2. My dad and I sometimes end our arguments calmly.

True   False   3. We almost never seem to agree.

True   False   4. I enjoy the talks we have.

True   False   5. When I state my own opinion, he gets upset.

True   False   6. At least three times a week, we get angry at each other.

True   False   7. My father listens when I need someone to talk to.

True   False   8. My dad is a good friend to me.

True   False   9. He says I have no consideration for him.

True   False   10. At least once a day we get angry at each other.

True   False   11. My father is bossy when we talk.

True   False   12. My dad understands me.

True   False   13. The talks we have are frustrating.

True   False   14. My dad understands my point of view, even when he doesn't agree with me.

True   False   15. My dad seems to be always complaining about me.

True   False   16. In general, I don't think we get along very well.

True   False   17. My dad yells a lot.

True   False   18. My dad puts me down.

True   False   19. If I run into problems, my dad helps me out.

True   False   20. I enjoy spending time with my father.

SCORING INSTRUCTIONS: CONFLICT BEHAVIOR QUESTIONNAIRE

This is a measure of communication—conflict behavior. The current 20-item version is a shortened revision, using item analysis procedures, of a longer 75-item version of the Conflict Behavior Questionnaire. A single score is obtained for each family member completing the questionnaire by following these guidelines. (Higher scores represent more negative communication.)

Parent Version

1. Add one point for each of the following items answered True: 5, 7, 8, 10, 11, 12, 13, 14, 15, 16, 17, 18, 19, 20.

2. Add one point for each of the following items answered False: 1, 2, 3, 4, 6, 9.

Adolescent Version

1. Add one point for each of the following items answered True: 1, 3, 5, 6, 9, 10, 11, 13, 15, 16, 17, 18.

2. Add one point for each of the following items answered False: 2, 4, 7, 8, 12, 14, 19, 20.

MEANS AND STANDARD DEVIATIONS FOR CBQ

Score	Distressed mean (SD)	Nondistressed mean (SD)	t	r-pb**
Mother	12.4 (5.0)	2.4 (2.8)	15.3*	.73
Father	10.5 (5.0)	3.2 (3.0)	5.2*	.51
Teen with mother	8.4 (6.0)	2.0 (3.1)	8.2*	.50
Teen with father	7.6 (5.4)	1.6 (1.6)	4.1*	.42

*$p < .001$
**Point biserial correlations between group membership and CBQ score.

T-SCORE CONVERSION TABLE FOR THE CONFLICT BEHAVIOR QUESTIONNAIRE–20

---

1. Locate the raw score for your family under the appropriate agent column (mom, dad, teen/mom, teen/dad).

2. Read the T-score in the next column to the right.

3. T-scores over 70 are clinically elevated.

Mom	T-score	Dad	T-score	Teen/Mom	T-score	Teen/Dad	T-score
0	41	0	39	0	44	0	40
1	45	1	43	1	47	1	46
2	49	2	46	2	50	2	53
3	52	3	49	3	53	3	59
4	56	4	53	4	56	4	65
5	59	5	56	5	60	5	71
6	63	6	59	6	63	6	78
7	66	7	63	7	66	7	84
8	70	8	66	8	69	8	90
9	74	9	69	9	73	9	96
10	77	10	70	10	76	10	103
11	81	11	73	11	79	11	109
12	84	12	76	12	82	12	115
13	88	13	79	13	85	13	121
14	91	14	83	14	89	14	128
15	95	15	86	15	92	15	134
16	99	16	89	16	95	16	140
17	102	17	93	17	98	17	146
18	106	18	96	18	102	18	153
19	109	19	99	19	105	19	159
20	113	20	116	20	136	20	136

Stimulant Drug Treatment Forms

These forms are provided so that physicians prescribing medication can provide appropriate information to parents about stimulant drugs and can obtain parents' written consent to have the child try these medications. Additional forms are provided to obtain important information about the side effects a child may experience during a drug trial. The physician's checklist is used at the time of the drug trial while the Follow-up Information form is used over the course of treatment for periodic monitoring of the child's response. The Side-Effects Rating Scale for stimulant medications can be mailed to teachers to complete as part of the drug trial.

PARENT INFORMATION SHEET ON STIMULANT DRUGS

The term *attention-deficit hyperactivity disorder* (ADHD) was introduced in 1987 in the new edition of the *Diagnostic and Statistical Manual—III-R,* published by the American Psychiatric Association. The change in terminology calls attention to the essential features of the syndrome: developmentally inappropriate inattention, impulsivity, and hyperactivity (when present). The confusion surrounding this entity is reflected in the variety of terms used in the past: hyperkinetic reaction of childhood, hyperkinetic syndrome, hyperactive child syndrome, minimal brain damage, minimal brain dysfunction (MBD), minimal cerebral dysfunction, minor cerebral dysfunction, and functional behavior problem (FBP), among others.

Associated or secondary features vary according to age and include obstinacy, stubbornness, negativism, bossiness, bullying, mood swings, excitability with a tendency to overreact, low frustration tolerance, temper outbursts, low self-esteem, and lack of response to discipline. Also encountered are coordination problems, speech impairment, perceptual disorders, and learning difficulties. ADHD is found in 3% of prepubertal children in the U.S., and is approximately 10 times more common in boys than in girls.

The onset of ADHD is typically by age 3, although frequently the disorder does not come to professional attention until the child enters school. Academic difficulties are common and social functioning is often impaired. Family patterns are disrupted by the child, and there is a fairly strong likelihood that one of the parents has, or had, ADHD (suggesting a genetic or hereditary pattern). In some cases the disorder is self-limited and disappears around puberty. In others it continues into adolescence and throughout adult life. With many, the hyperactivity disappears at a certain point, but the attention problems and impulsivity persist.

DRUGS USED FOR ADHD

I. Stimulant Drugs
  A. Amphetamines
    Amphetamine
    Dextroamphetamine
    Methamphetamine
    Benzedrine®
    Dexedrine®
    Desoxyn®, Methedrine®
  B. Non-Amphetamines
    Methylphenidate
    Pemoline
    Ritalin®
    Cylert®
II. Antidepressant Drugs
    Imipramine
    Tofranil®

DRUG TREATMENT

The history of stimulant drug use dates back to the discovery by Bradley in 1937 of the therapeutic effects of Benzedrine® on behaviorally disturbed children. In 1948, Dexedrine® was introduced, with the advantage of having equal efficacy at half the dose. Ritalin® was released in 1954 with the hope that it would have fewer side effects and less abuse potential. Although they were initially also popular as antidepressants and diet pills, stimulant drugs are rarely used for those purposes today.

In 1957, Laufer described the "hyperkinetic impulse disorder," which he believed was caused by a maturational lag in the development of the central nervous system. He asserted that stimulant drugs were the treatment of choice for this disorder, and postulated that they acted by stimulating the midbrain, placing it in a more synchronous balance with the outer cerebral cortex. This was an oversimplification, but the exact mechanism of action of these drugs is still unknown.

The most frequently used of the stimulant drugs is Ritalin®, followed by Dexedrine®, Desoxyn®, Benzedrine®, and Cylert®. Dexedrine®, Benzedrine®, and Desoxyn® are amphetamine preparations; Ritalin® and Cylert® are nonamphetamines. Cylert® works differently from the other drugs, taking 2–4 weeks before therapeutic effects are noted. Tofranil® is an antidepressant that is also used to treat bedwetting, panic disorders, school phobia, and ADHD. Various dietary programs have been attempted, including the Feingold program (curtailing food additives), low sugar diets, vegetarian diets, etc. None of these dietary regimens have proven to be successful when put to careful scientific scrutiny.

MODE OF DRUG ACTION

It is postulated that stimulant drugs act by affecting the catecholamine neurotransmitters (especially dopamine) in the brain. Some believe that ADHD develops from a dopamine deficiency, which can be corrected by stimulant drug treatment. At one time it was felt that the stimulant drugs created a paradoxical (opposite and unexpected) reaction (calming and sedation) in ADHD youngsters, and that this response was diagnostic. This is no longer believed to be the case, as the response to stimulant drugs is neither paradoxical, nor specific. Children with conduct disorders and no evidence of ADHD may also respond to these drugs. Likewise, studies with normal and enuretic (bedwetting) children have shown that many experience a calming effect rather than the expected stimulation.

Because of their relative safety, the stimulant drugs remain the treatment of choice in treating ADHD. The drugs are unquestionably successful in decreasing hyperactivity, lessening impulsivity, and improving attention span in approximately 70% of those treated. As a result of improved interactions with family members, peers, and teachers, the drug-treated children feel better about themselves, and self-esteem rises. At the present time, however, there is some controversy as to the degree of learning and memory improvement resulting from the treatment of ADHD children with stimulant drugs. Overall, the ideal approach is one in which the children are involved in individual, group, or family therapy, along with drug treatment.

CONTRAINDICATIONS

1. Known hypersensitivity or allergic reaction to the drug.
2. Seizure history.
3. Glucoma.
4. Hypertension.
5. History of tics.
6. Hyperthyroidism.
7. Pregnancy.

DRUG INTERACTIONS

The drugs may decrease the effects of some antihypertensive drugs (e.g., Ismelin®). They should be used cautiously with pressor agents (adrenalin-like drugs). They may affect the liver metabolism of certain anticoagulants, anticonvulsants, and tricyclic antidepressants. Insulin requirements in diabetic patients may be altered when the drugs are co-mixed.

PRESCRIBING INFORMATION

Ritalin® is available in 5, 10, and 20 mg tablets. A new preparation, Ritalin-SR®, is a sustained-release product with effects lasting 6–8 hours (twice as long as the standard preparation). The usual starting dosage of the standard Ritalin® for children under 8 is a single 5 mg tablet in the morning, and for children over 8 is a single 10 mg tablet in the morning. Each week the daily dosage can be increased by 5 mg and 10 mg a day, respectively. Usually the tablets are taken at breakfast and lunch; occasionally an after-school dose is necessary. The tablets should be taken on an empty stomach, ½ hour before or after meals. The total maximum dosage should not exceed 60 mg, although under extreme situations 80 mg/day dosages are prescribed.

There has been little experience with the sustained-release SR® preparation. One study showed that it was as effective as the shorter-acting preparation, and had no difference in side effects. The SR® preparation comes in 20 mg tablets, roughly equal to two of the standard 10 mg tablets taken 4 hours apart. Generally, the initial dosage adjustments are done with the standard preparation, which is later switched to the SR® brand for maintenance treatment.

The amphetamines are quite similar in their pharmacologic makeup. Dexedrine® comes in 5, 10, and 15 mg tablets and capsules; in a liquid elixir preparation with 5 mg per teaspoon; and in slow-release capsules of 5, 10, and 15 mg. The dosage is approximately half that of Ritalin®. Benzedrine is available in 5, 10, and 15 mg tablets; and in a 15 mg sustained-release capsule. The dosage range is similar to Dexedrine® (5–60 mg/day). Desoxyn® is available in 2.5 and 5 mg tablets; and in 5, 10, and 15 mg sustained-release capsules. Pharmacological actions are similar to those of Dexedrine® and Benzedrine®.

Cylert® is given once a day, giving it an advantage over the shorter-acting preparations. It has a gradual onset of action; significant clinical benefits may not be evident until the 3rd or 4th week of treatment, and they may take as long as 6 weeks. The drug is available in 18.75, 37.5, and 75 mg tablets; and in 37.5 mg chewable tablets. The recommended starting dose is 37.5 mg, and the dosage is increased in daily increments of 18.75 mg per week until the desired clinical effects are reached. The effective daily dose for most patients is in the range between 56.25–75 mg. The maximum daily dose is 112.5 mg.

Of those ADHD-children treated with stimulant drugs, 66%–75% will improve and 5%–10% will get worse. It is always important to verify that the medication is actually being taken, as some children will refuse to do so as a means of rebellion or defiance. There is a marked variation in drug response among different children, and even within an individual child on different days. Some children will not respond unless they are placed on extremely high doses, or on 4–5 doses a day, probably as a result of accelerated metabolism (drug breakdown).

Tolerance to the stimulant drugs may develop, requiring an increase in dosage after the child has maintained nicely on a particular dosage for a year or so. Children who respond to one of these stimulant drugs will probably respond as well to any of the others. There are cases, however, in which a child will respond favorably to one drug but not another. Also, there is no evidence that children treated for years with stimulant drugs will have a greater likelihood of abusing drugs or narcotics during their adolescent years.

SIDE EFFECTS

The most common side effects encountered with stimulant drugs are: loss of appetite, weight loss, sleeping problems, irritability, restlessness, stomachache, headache, rapid heart rate, elevated blood pressure, sudden deterioration of behavior, and symptoms of depression with sadness, crying, and withdrawn behavior. Two of the most disconcerting side effects are the intensification of tics (muscle twitches of the face and other parts of the body), and suppression of growth. It is rare that stimulant drugs cause tics, but they may activate an underlying (latent) tic condition. There is some concern that this could even lead to a severe tic condition called Tourette's Syndrome. As a result, ADHD children with tics are often treated with the neuroleptic tranquilizer, Haldol®, either alone or in combination with one of the stimulant drugs (Benzedrine® may be the safest under these circumstances).

The growth retardation problem has caused considerable controversy and concern since an article written in 1972 described suppression in growth of ADHD children who had undergone long-term stimulant drug treatment. Subsequent studies have varied markedly in their findings. One study of adolescents who took the drugs as children showed no growth suppression. Another study demonstrated growth suppression during the 1st year, but none during the 2nd year of drug treatment. Others have demonstrated a rebound growth spurt when the drug is withdrawn, or even in those still taking the medication. There is also some indication that taller children are more vulnerable to growth suppression effects than are those who are smaller. The problems appear to be dose-related, occurring in Dexedrine® doses of 15 mg or more per day, and Ritalin® doses greater than 30–40 mg per day. Experts now believe that any risk of growth suppression in most children is minimal and is mainly in body weight rather than height. Even the effects on weight are small, averaging approximately 2 pounds during the first year.

As a result of the growth retardation scare, many clinicians are suggesting that the drugs be given only on school days and not on weekends, holidays, or vacations. Realistically, most parents are unable to tolerate the deterioration in behavior that ensues when the medication is withdrawn. At the very least, the drugs should be withdrawn once a year to reestablish the need to continue the medication. A popular approach is to discontinue the stimulant drugs during the first 2 weeks of November. If the medication is still required, it will be apparent soon enough, and not too late to endanger the child's grades and reputation among schoolmates and teachers.

Other rare side effects include: irregular heartbeat, hair loss, decreased white blood cell count, anemia, and rash. Elevated liver function tests may be associated with Cylert®. A rare hypersensitivity reaction consists of hives, fever, and easy bruising. Occasionally, ADHD children on stimulant drugs will experience a personality change characterized by dejection, lifelessness, tearfulness, and oversensitivity. Conversely, some may develop a state of excitement, confusion, and withdrawal.

PARENT CONSENT FORM FOR STIMULANT DRUGS

I am aware that my child is taking a stimulant drug as a necessary part of his/her treatment program for Attention Deficit Disorder (ADD). I have been informed either verbally, or from written material, of: (1) a general idea as to how the medication works; (2) the typical dosage range; (3) contraindications; (4) interactions with other drugs; (5) possible side effects; and (6) toxic effects of the drug. I am aware of the following facts related to the drug:

1. In the cases of Ritalin®, Dexedrine®, Desoxyn®, and Benzedrine® the therapeutic effects may be experienced within a matter of hours or days. With Cylert® it may take up to 2–6 weeks before beneficial results are attained. In some cases the drugs will be ineffective in treating ADD.

2. Commonly encountered side effects include: loss of appetite, weight loss, sleeping problems, irritability, restlessness, stomachache, headache, rapid heart rate, and elevated blood pressure.

3. The drugs may exacerbate (bring about) a latent tic (facial twitch) condition. There is a possibility that in predisposed children these drugs could bring about the development of Tourette's Syndrome, a severe condition of facial tics, obscene utterances, and other bizarre behaviors.

4. The drugs may affect growth. Studies do not agree in this area, however. The safest approach is to keep dosage to a minimum, using the drugs only when necessary and taking the child off the medication periodically (perhaps once a year) to corroborate the need to continue.

5. Other rare side effects include: irregular heartbeat, hair loss, decreased white blood cell (WBC) count, anemia, and rash. Elevated liver function tests have been reported with Cylert®. A rare hypersensitivity reaction consists of hives, fever, and easy bruising. Occasionally ADD children on stimulant drugs will experience a personality change manifested by dejection, lifelessness, tearfulness, and oversensitivity. Conversely, some develop a state of excitement, confusion, and withdrawal.

6. Children taking stimulant drugs need to make regular visits to the prescribing physician to monitor dosage, check side effects, and perform any laboratory tests or procedures deemed necessary.

Date _____   Signature _____

SSN _____   Witness _____

I elect to waive informed consent:

Date _____   Signature _____

SSN _____   Witness _____

PHYSICIAN'S CHECKLIST FOR PARENTS

Name _____ Birthdate _____ Current Age _____ Sex: M__ F__

Date of Evaluation _____ . Relationship _____ .

Instructions: This checklist of questions should be reviewed monthly with parents of children taking stimulant drugs.

1. What dose have you been regularly giving to this child over the past month?

   Medication: _____ Dose: _____

2. Have you noticed any of the following side effects this month?

☐ loss of appetite/weight
☐ insomnia
☐ irritability in late morning or late afternoon
☐ unusual crying
☐ tics or nervous habits
☐ headache/stomachache
☐ sadness
☐ rashes
☐ dizziness
☐ dark circles under eyes
☐ fearfulness
☐ social withdrawal
☐ drowsiness
☐ anxiety

3. If so, please decribe how often and when the side effects occurred. _____
   _____

4. Have you spoken with the child's teacher lately? How is the child performing in class? ___
   _____

5. Did your child complain about taking the medication or avoid its use? _____
   _____

6. Does the drug seem to be helping the child as much this month as it did last month? If not, what seems to have changed? _____
   _____

7. When was your child last examined by the doctor? (If more than 1 year, schedule the child for a clinic visit and exam.) _____
   _____

8. Have there been problems in giving the child medication at school? _____
   _____

Note. From *Hyperactive Children: A Handbook for Diagnosis and Treatment* by R. A. Barkley, 1981, New York: Guilford Press. Copyright 1981 by The Guilford Press. A Division of Guilford Publications, Inc. This form may be reproduced for personal use.

FOLLOW-UP INFORMATION

Name _____ Birthdate _____ Current Age _____ Sex: M__ F__

Medication: _____

Parents' attitudes about medication: _____

Teacher's attitude about medication: _____

Child's attitude about medication: _____

Problems: _____

_____

History: Target symptoms	Improved	No change	Worse
Hyperactivity—motor restlessness	☐	☐	☐
Attention span	☐	☐	☐
Distractibility	☐	☐	☐
Finishing tasks	☐	☐	☐
Impulse control	☐	☐	☐
Frustration tolerance	☐	☐	☐
Accepting limits	☐	☐	☐
Peer relations	☐	☐	☐

Side effects			
Appetite	☐	☐	☐
Sleep	☐	☐	☐
Elimination	☐	☐	☐
Weepiness	☐	☐	☐
Drowsiness	☐	☐	☐
Mouth dryness	☐	☐	☐
Abdominal complaints	☐	☐	☐
Others	☐	☐	☐

Physical examination

Height _____

Weight _____

B.P. _____

P. _____

Positive findings _____

_____

WBC _____ Other lab tests: _____ Date done: _____

Impression

_____

_____

_____

_____

R$_x$ _____

Return date: _____.

SIDE EFFECTS RATING SCALE

Name _____ **Date** _____

Person Completing This Form _____

Instructions: Please rate each behavior from 0 (absent) to 9 (serious). Circle only one number beside each item. A zero means that you have not seen the behavior in this child during the past week, and a 9 means that you have noticed it and believe it to be either very serious or to occur very frequently.

Behavior	Absent									Serious
Insomnia or trouble sleeping	0	1	2	3	4	5	6	7	8	9
Nightmares	0	1	2	3	4	5	6	7	8	9
Stares a lot or daydreams	0	1	2	3	4	5	6	7	8	9
Talks less with others	0	1	2	3	4	5	6	7	8	9
Uninterested in others	0	1	2	3	4	5	6	7	8	9
Decreased appetite	0	1	2	3	4	5	6	7	8	9
Irritable	0	1	2	3	4	5	6	7	8	9
Stomachaches	0	1	2	3	4	5	6	7	8	9
Headaches	0	1	2	3	4	5	6	7	8	9
Drowsiness	0	1	2	3	4	5	6	7	8	9
Sad/unhappy	0	1	2	3	4	5	6	7	8	9
Prone to crying	0	1	2	3	4	5	6	7	8	9
Anxious	0	1	2	3	4	5	6	7	8	9
Bites fingernails	0	1	2	3	4	5	6	7	8	9
Euphoric/unusually happy	0	1	2	3	4	5	6	7	8	9
Dizziness	0	1	2	3	4	5	6	7	8	9
Tics or nervous movements	0	1	2	3	4	5	6	7	8	9

Note. From *Hyperactive Children: A Handbook for Diagnosis and Treatment* by R. A. Barkley, 1981, New York: Guilford Press. Copyright 1981 by The Guilford Press. A Division of Guilford Publications, Inc. This form may be reproduced for personal use.

Daily Home–School Report Cards

One method for increasing the behavior management of ADHD children at school is to use information from the teacher as part of a home-based reward program. Instructions for setting up a daily report card system are provided along with three sample report cards we have used. The behaviors to be rated on the cards can be changed to suit the particular target behaviors of interest in a specific case.

INSTRUCTIONS FOR USE OF THE DAILY HOME–SCHOOL REPORT CARD

What follows is an example of how to use the daily report card that you have been provided by our clinic for use with your child. As you can see from the cards, this system is designed to give you, the parent, daily information on your child's performance in a variety of areas of academic functioning from all of his or her teachers.

Every day your child should take this card to school with him or her and give it to each of his or her teachers that day. The card should be given to the teacher at the end of each class period. The teacher is then to mark on the card a number rating to indicate how well or how poorly the child did that day in each area noted on the card. The areas on the card involve class participation, classwork, homework, and interactions with other children. After rating the child, the teacher is to initial it at the bottom of the column underneath his or her ratings. This is to insure that these are indeed the teacher's

ratings. The child receives a number from 1 to 5: 1 represents excellent, performance in that area, 2 represents good, 3 represents fair, 4 represents poor performance, and 5 indicates that the child was terrible or did not function at all well in that particular area that day. There is space on the card for up to six teachers to evaluate the child each day. At the end of school, the child is to return the card home.

When the child comes home, the parents should first look over the card and provide the child with praise should the card contain mostly ratings of 1, 2, or 3. If the child's marks are particularly poor, the parent should question the child at that time as to the reason for the poor performance.

After this discussion, the parent should assign points for each number that is on the card. The points should be assigned as follows:

Rating		Points
1	=	25
2	=	15
3	=	5
4	=	−15
5	=	−25

After adding up the points that the child has received or lost that day, the parent then tells the child how many points they have earned for that school day. As you can see from the rating, if a child receives a 1 and a 5 on the card, they will cancel each other out and the child will receive 0 points. This insures that the child is penalized for any bad ratings and is rewarded for every good rating on the card. The child is to use the total points for that day to purchase his or her privileges around the home.

When it is convenient, the parent and child should sit down together and make up a list of household privileges and assign point values to those privileges. The following list is meant only as a suggestion to the parent and child as to how to make this list.

Points needed		Activity or privilege
30 points	=	½ hour of television
30 points	=	playing outside after school
20 points	=	snack while watching television
50 points	=	½ hour past usual bedtime on weekend
150 points	=	for movie
150 points	=	trip to McDonald's restaurant

Once a list such as the above is made, the child will then know how he or she can exchange points for the various household privileges. On a day when a child earns no points, the child is simply allowed to read a book or play in his room, but does not have access to television or playing outdoors.

In some cases, children will intentionally lose a card or will intentionally forget to obtain a teacher's rating if their performance in school that day, or in that particular class, was especially poor. In this case, the child is to lose 500 points for failing to bring the card home on any given day. Anytime the child forgets to receive a teacher's evaluation, the child is to lose 150 points for every teacher missed on the card.

Almost all children find this system to be quite rewarding after they have used it for several days. In fact, many become quite stingy or miserly about spending their points, and will often give up watching television rather than spend the points on this particular privilege. In addition, many begin to develop a new attitude toward school because of their ability to earn extra privileges by performing well in school on any particular day. Thus, this program is a quite positive program for most children rather than a punitive one.

We have found that some children are able to save up a substantial amount of points towards the purchase of future gifts, toys, or special activities, such as a trip to an amusement park. This is fine. However, when the points that the child is saving become quite substantial, the child may feel that he can goof off in school for one or two days and obtain bad ratings, yet still have enough points in his savings account to purchase his privileges that day. To avoid this problem, we require that a child use the points he earned that day to purchase the privileges he wants to use that day. Any points left over are put towards a future savings account which the child cannot go into simply to buy daily activities such as watching television or going outside. Therefore, if a child brings home a poor daily report card, he is not able to use his savings account points to buy privileges that day, but must suffer the consequences for his poor report card.

Some parents ask if this report card does not single out the child for individual teasing and criticism from his peers at school. We have rarely found this to be the case. Instead, we often find the children become quite proud of their report card especially if it contains very positive evaluations from their teachers. In fact, we have found that other students have called, asking if they too can use this system. The child's pride over the report card also develops because he is able to purchase many extra privileges that his friends are unable to obtain, because of his excellent performance in school.

Should you have any questions about our daily report card system please feel free to ask the clinic staff member who is working with you and your child. If you are ever in doubt as to how much a privilege should cost in points, we generally suggest that each point be worth 2¢ and that this be used when deciding how much a gift, toy, or other object should be worth in points. For instance a movie generally costing $4.00 to attend would require that the child have 200 points before he could see that movie.

We believe you will be quite successful in using this program.

DAILY STUDENT RATING CARD

NAME _____ DATE _____

Please rate this child in each of the areas listed below as to how he performed in school today using ratings of 1 to 5. 1 = excellent, 2 = good, 3 = fair, 4 = poor, 5 = terrible or did not work.

Area	Class periods/Subjects					
	1	2	3	4	5	6
participation						
class work						
handed in homework						
interaction with other children						
teacher's initials						

Place comments on back if needed:

DAILY HOME–SCHOOL REPORT CARD—RECESS

Name _____   **Date** _____

Please evaluate this child in the following areas of behavior during free or unstructured school time, especially during *recess*. Using a rating of 1 = excellent, 2 = good, 3 = fair, 4 = poor, please place a number beside each behavior listed below for each recess or free-time period this child is observed each day.

Free Time/Recess

	#1	#2	#3	#4
1. Keeps hands to self; does not push, shove, pinch, or touch others wrongly	—	—	—	—
2. Does not fight with other children (hitting, kicking, biting) or try to provoke them by tripping them, shoving them, or taking their things	—	—	—	—
3. Follows rules	—	—	—	—
4. Tries to get along well with other children	—	—	—	—

Other comments:

DAILY HOME–SCHOOL REPORT CARD—CLASS BEHAVIOR

Name _____ **Date** _____

Please rate the student in each of the areas of classroom behavior and attention using the scale from 1 (excellent) to 5 (poor). Place your rating beside each item in the column corresponding to your class period. Please initial at the bottom of your column to verify your ratings.

			Class Period				
	1	2	3	4	5	6	7

Behavior

1. Has materials needed to begin class work (clean paper, pencil, proper textbook, no unnecessary materials on desk, has homework ready to hand in)

	___	___	___	___	___	___	___

2. Pays attention to speaker during class lectures and discussions (looks at person speaking, avoids playing with objects, doodling, or getting off-task)

	___	___	___	___	___	___	___

3. Takes notes during class lectures and discussions (writes down at least 5 notes during class discussions, copies all math from board)

	___	___	___	___	___	___	___

4. Participates in class discussions (asks and answers at least 1 question each class)

	___	___	___	___	___	___	___

5. Keeps work materials neat, organized, and in proper place (papers in correct section of notebook, homework assignments in homework notebook, etc.)

	___	___	___	___	___	___	___

Teacher's initials, please

	___	___	___	___	___	___	___

Homework: (Have student write homework below if this is helpful.)

Study Skills Checklist for Homework

I designed this form to use as part of an intervention program for helping ADHD children and adolescents to concentrate better during their studies. The form is kept beside the child while doing homework as a reminder of what skills to use while studying. The parent can then rate the child's use of each skill. These ratings could then be used in a home reward program where the child earns privileges for how well he or she adheres to these study skills.

STUDY SKILLS CHECKLIST FOR HOMEWORK

Please place this sheet in front of your child while he or she is doing homework. Have him or her review it each evening before starting homework. When the homework is completed, review it and evaluate how well your child followed these directions. Rate each of the five areas below using a rating from 1 (excellent) to 5 (poor) below each item where it says Parent Evaluation.

1. Read each direction carefully. Then underline the *action* words in each direction (add, subtract, write, solve, etc.).
   Parent evaluation _____

2. Put a check mark beside a direction when you feel you understand the instructions.
   Parent evaluation _____

3. If you do not understand a passage you have read, try to read it again. If you still don't understand it, ask your parents for assistance.
   Parent evaluation _____

4. Once you have finished your work, read it over and then place a check mark next to each answer on the page to show that you have read it over and checked for accuracy.
   Parent evaluation _____

5. In social studies and language, expand your answers to full sentences. Do not use brief phrases to answer questions. Place a check mark next to your answer to show that you know it is a complete sentence or idea.
   Parent evaluation _____